D0493511

For Ewan and Florence . . . I did it all for you.

PENGUIN BOOKS

UK | USA | Canada | Ireland | Australia
India | New Zealand | South Africa

Penguin Books is part of the Penguin Random House group of companies
whose addresses can be found at global.penguinrandomhouse.com.

www.penguin.co.uk   www.puffin.co.uk   www.ladybird.co.uk

Penguin
Random House
UK

First published 2020

004

Text and additional photography copyright © Daisy Upton, 2020
Photography by Cristina Pedreira Pérez
Photography copyright © Cristina Pedreira Pérez, 2020
Illustrations © Shutterstock
Additional photographs by Daisy Upton

The moral right of the author and photographer has been asserted

Text design by Janene Spencer
Printed and bound in Latvia

A CIP catalogue record for this book is available from the British Library

ISBN: 978–0–241–44362–0

All correspondence to:
Penguin Books
Penguin Random House Children's
80 Strand, London WC2R 0RL

Five Minute Mum

Daisy Upton

GIVE ME FIVE

PENGUIN BOOKS

CONTENTS

INTRODUCTION

Let me tell you a story, if you'll be so kind as to indulge me for a moment.

It was January 2018. The coldest winter in thirty-something years. (I should remember – the weather reporters banged on about it for months.) After seeing out the festivities of New Year's Eve with a hearty bang, I rapidly came down with what was dubbed 'Aussie flu'. Now, even under normal circumstances, the flu is utter rubbish, but I was at home with three-year-old Ewan and one-year-old Florence. All day. They wanted to be entertained, and they didn't care that Mummy felt like her eyeballs were going to explode, or that she'd just been sick in the kitchen sink.

It was too cold to go outside so, in my delirious and sorry state, I decided we should make papier mâché hot-air balloons. (I know – what was I thinking?)

I will blow up balloons and the kids can spend a decent hour sticking strips of newspaper to them, then they can paint them. That'll keep them busy, I foolishly thought.

So I set to work gathering equipment. I attempted to fashion something to stand the balloons up on. I tore up loads of strips of newspaper and mixed up the gluey paste. It took me the best part of forty minutes, and all the while the kids fidgeted and fought at my feet, asking relentless questions.

And how long did they do the papier mâché for?

Well, Florence lasted two minutes and ten seconds. After four and a half minutes, Ewan sighed and said, 'Can I watch telly now?'

I completed the papier mâché on my own.

When I asked them to paint the balloons the following day, the same thing happened: they had zero interest in the activity. And then I had to clean it all up . . . My exhausted, feverish heart shattered into a thousand pieces. **'THIS. IS. TOO. HARD!'** I wanted to scream. **'THIS. IS. TOO. HARD!'**

There had to be other easier things I could do with them. They'd learned nothing from this balloon experience, except that Mummy would finish it off once they were bored. I hadn't even managed to knock back a Lemsip in peace!

Once I had recovered from the flu and was back to my old self, I set to work. I'm a qualified teaching assistant, and I have experience teaching classes of thirty children from nursery age up to six years old. I've had specialist training and worked with children with dyslexia and speech and language difficulties. I might no longer have been working in that setting, but I now had two children under four of my own. Surely I could think of some games that we could play together.

Games that wouldn't take long to set up, or be messy. Games that we could *all* get something out of.

So that's exactly what I did. I came up with ideas that would keep my little ones occupied, but wouldn't take away a part of my sanity. Activities for those days when you just aren't feeling up to parenting, or when you just need five minutes, or when you want to be fun but just haven't got much time. Games that can be set up in no more than five minutes, and that use stuff you already have around the house (not a glue gun, seventy-five empty loo rolls and an upside-down dining table, like the 'kids' Pinterest board I had saved). Ideas that are fun for both you and your little ones. Activities with education at their heart, but in such a way that it never feels like it.

I wrote down all the different games I invented. Some were from my teaching days, when I was inspired by children with unique learning challenges. Some I learned from incredible colleagues (mainly those at Irlam Endowed Primary School – thanks, guys) who showed me that early-years education should be simple and child-led, because that is always best. Some just popped into my head while I was doing something else with my kids, or when I was in the shower with two little nudies splashing at my feet.

The ideas came spilling out. I shared them with friends, and they shared them with their friends, and I began to realize that there might just be a wider need for this. I was lucky enough to have trained in early-years education before I had my own children, but how many other parents ever get taught how to play? Where's the antenatal class that explains how to introduce the alphabet to your child? Or how to set up toys so your kid is engaged for more than thirty seconds? Or how to play 'making cups of tea and pretend cakes' for more than three minutes without questioning your life choices? That class simply doesn't exist.

And what about all the parents who work part-time or full-time and want to do meaningful activities when they are with their kids but feel like there just isn't time?

Who *does* have the time to set up elaborate papier mâché hot-air balloon activities?

No one. That's who. Imaginary 'perfect' parents we all sort of aspire to be but, really, if we admit it we're all just a bit too tired to become. (And our houses are already ruined enough, thank you very much.)

So here I am, Five Minute Mum, with a book full of ideas for those tricky toddler to preschool years alongside a healthy dose of reality. Each idea takes no more than five minutes to set up because then I know that if it doesn't work, and gets the old toddler two fingers or induces a mighty tantrum, it doesn't matter. It will only take me five minutes to put it all away again. My rage is kept at bay. But, if it *does* work, my little one might play for five minutes or more. They might learn something new. I might get to drink my brew in one fell swoop. Or we will laugh together, and I will feel fan-freaking-tastic about myself as a parent. #winning

My games are easy. They use stuff you will probably already have at home – and, if you don't, I always give alternatives. Some are designed to be played together, so you feel you have easily joined in on the fun. Some are designed to entertain your wee person independently for five minutes, so you can nip out to the loo in peace (the dream!).

When I started my blog off the back of the 2018 Aussie flu balloon fiasco, I never thought it would get to where it is today. I am so incredibly thrilled it has. I'm always delighted to hear from other people who just want to know that they are doing OK at this parenting malarkey, even if they feel like they never have time to cover all bases. I feel the same.

So, I wrote down these games for you. On the days when you think you're failing at every turn, you can pick up this book of quick and easy ideas, choose one, and perhaps turn a bad day into a good one. Because, as we all know with little kids, your day can turn on a sixpence and sometimes five minutes is all you need.

LANGUAGE, PLEASE . . .

Those of you who are avid readers of my blog might notice that the language in this book is a little 'toned down', shall we say? That isn't because I don't still whisper the old effs and jeffs to myself out of kid earshot on a daily basis, because I do. Quite frankly, parenting brings out the Billy Connolly in the best of us. However, unlike my blog, this book is designed to be left knocking around where little hands will get hold of it. And, as keen as I am to help your wee folk learn how to sound out words, I really don't want their first reading experience to be them asking you, 'I can see the "sh" sound in this word, but what does it say?'

So the language has been knocked down a peg or two, and instead I popped in the kind of alternatives we holler when we stub our toe, begin screaming 'OH MY –' then spot our two-year-old staring at us and finish with 'FULLULAH GAWD'. Oh and 'WTAF' obviously stands for 'what the actual fudgeballs' (winky face emoji).

HOW TO USE THIS BOOK

This book contains fun ideas for things to do with little kids aged from one to five. The activities cover lots of skills on the UK's Early Years Foundation Stage (EYFS) curriculum. I know – BORING! All this means is that my games secretly involve all kinds of skills that will help with your child's development (in your face, stupid aged-two questionnaire!). So, when you play these games with your kids, you can feel positively superhero-esque, because you're ticking off all the important bits and having a laugh together. An easy win? Yes please.

On the first page of each game, you'll find a little set of tabs that give a rough idea of the sort of skills the game promotes and the appropriate age for players. These tabs are just a guide; you don't have to adhere to them religiously. Likewise, the ages are only there to help you out – if your one-year-old wants to join in with a game for the over-threes, that's fine (and the same goes if it's the other way round).

SAFETY BITS AND BOBS

Now a lot of this is common sense stuff but I want to highlight some safety things, because I don't know about you but when I've had zero sleep (for years) even the most basic of safety measures can slip my addled brain. So here are a few bits and bobs to consider when playing the games in this book:

■ **MAGNETIC LETTERS AND NUMBERS** are for over-threes only. They have those tiny magnets in the back that can sometimes pop out, and if a little one swallows those it can be very dangerous. So keep them out of reach of the wee ones.

■ We love **GAMES WHERE YOU MOVE AND JUMP ABOUT**, and obviously when it's chucking it down again we play these inside. I eventually got rid of our coffee table because the stress of its corners was just too much. So, before you play any of those energetic games indoors, just have a quick check about for any sharp edges or corners and move well away or find a way to make them safe.

■ And finally **WATER** . . . even the shallowest bowl of the wet stuff can be a drowning risk for little ones. So, if you're playing any games with water, watch like a hawk. I mean, have a brew in your hand by all means, but use the time to just watch them at play. It's proper lovely when they are happily splashing – like having your own baby water feature!

HERE'S AN OVERVIEW OF WHAT THOSE TABS MEAN:

 Age: This is based on the age at which my kids were happy to try each game. Lots of the activities in the first four chapters are for children over two, but the last chapter, 'Quick Ideas For . . .', is full of ideas for one-year-olds.

 Gross motor skills: This just means 'big movement' skills – stuff like running, jumping, throwing and balancing.

 Fine motor skills: The opposite of gross motor skills. Little movements that are usually done sitting down, such as gripping a pencil or threading with a bit of string.

 Speech: All my games promote speaking! The ones with this tab are particularly good for encouraging your little ones to talk.

 Mark–making: This is teacherspeak for putting pen to paper, and it's what kids do before they learn to write. Games with this tab will encourage your little ones to have a go at squiggling.

 Numbers: These games have a number focus, although you could play many of them with letters too if you fancied – or with anything else, for that matter!

 Letters: These games encourage letter recognition, but again they are all quite adaptable and you could play them with numbers, words or anything else.

FIVE MINUTE KIT

In the majority of cases, I hope that you'll be able to pick up this book at any given moment and play plenty of the games simply using stuff you already have knocking around the house. That is how I always play, and it's how I am inspired to think up new games. I just ask, 'What can I grab to play with?' Kids are expensive as it is, so the less extra stuff you have to buy the better!

However, you might want to pull together a bit of a survival kit to have on hand for coping with long school holidays and rainy days. So here are some of the things that I use regularly, along with some toys that I think make good investments because your kids will play with them over and over.

FROM THE STATIONERY BOX
- pens and pencils
- chalk
- assorted coloured paper and card
- masking tape
- scissors (a pair for you, plus some child-friendly ones)
- paper clips
- Post-its (or any other sticky notes)
- whiteboard markers
- chalk pens and/or paint sticks

FROM THE KITCHEN AND UTILITY ROOM
- plastic cups
- various utensils – spoons, spatulas, etc.
- small trays with raised edges (IKEA is a great place to get these!)
- a muffin tray or a baking tin
- tinfoil
- buckets or washing baskets

FROM THE 'ODDS AND ENDS' DRAWER
- balloons
- Blu-Tack (or any other sticky tack)
- dice
- reusable straws
- pegs
- string
- glow sticks

FROM THE RECYCLING BIN

- old newspapers
- cardboard boxes of assorted sizes
- plastic bottles with their lids
- old formula or washing-powder canisters with little plastic scoops

INVESTMENT TOYS (THE ONES I USE A LOT!)

- puzzles and puzzle boards
- assorted wooden blocks
- anything featuring letters and numbers – wooden puzzles, foam letters and numbers for the bath, foam mats you can stand on, magnetic ones, etc. (Try to have both upper-case and lower-case letters, but if you have to choose go with lower-case as this is what we see more regularly when reading.)
- a variety of balls – small ones, bouncy ones, ping-pong balls, footballs, etc.
- small teddies, soft toys and dolls
- play dough
- something you can write on and instantly wipe clean, such as a whiteboard, blackboard or Magna Doodle
- toy cars, trains, diggers, trucks and other vehicles
- play sand (kinetic sand is excellent!)
- a toy tea set
- Duplo (or any other sets with chunky building bricks)
- musical instruments
- play food
- toy doctor's kit
- toy toolbox

You should have most of this stuff already, if not all of it, and I suggest alternatives wherever I can so you don't need to buy anything extra to use this book. But in case it's handy I've made a shopping list of where I get my kit, so please see my website if you want links to anything specific that you're missing.

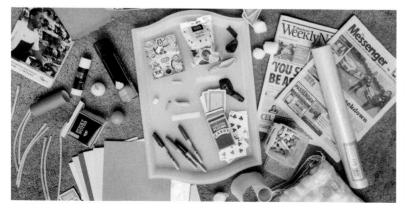

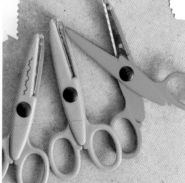

THE GOLDEN RULE

So here it is. My only rule. A golden one. I use it for **EVERY SINGLE GAME** we play.

ALWAYS LET THE KIDS COME TO THE GAME.

Try not to clap your hands and say, 'OK, kids, we are going to do this incredible activity now!' Even if you use your best, most Oscar-worthy 'This is going to be awesome!' voice, they will **KNOW**. They just know.

In their little heads, they will think, *Yep, you're trying to teach me something. I'm not having it. No chance. This bit of cardboard that's been on the floor for three days has suddenly taken my interest.*

Or, as was the case with the balloon fiasco, they'll wrestle at your feet and fire questions at you faster than a quiz-show host. Meanwhile, you will just get more and more flustered and have to try very hard not to shout, 'Can you just buzz off for two damn minutes while I set up this **VERY FUN** activity?!'

So, what *do* you do, then?

Here's what: you set up the activity while they are busy elsewhere or asleep or out of the house (obviously at childcare, not just popping into town for some bits), and then you **LEAVE IT**. Just leave it there for them to find and say, 'What's this?' Then you can just casually reply, 'It's a game. Do you want to play?' And so it begins.

Alternatively, if you do want to encourage your kids, don't say anything. Instead, when you're ready, just start to play yourself. Then, when they approach, ask them, 'Do you want to play too?'

Once you've got their interest, you can explain what to do. It is crucial at this point to try to do something **SILLY**. Get it wrong yourself, laugh, make a funny noise or do a crazy voice. Engage your child at their level of fun. You want them to think, *I want to play this too!* In teacherspeak this is called child-led play, but in parent speak it is, 'Let them think they are in control because if I tell them what to do they will go freaking bananas.' By letting your child make the decision to join in, you are allowing them to lead the way. This empowers them and also takes the pressure off trying to engage them.

So that's the GOLDEN RULE: never force it.

If your kids come, great. If they don't? Leave the activity out if you can. They might approach it later. They might not. It doesn't matter. It's only five minutes.

OLD FAVOURITES REIMAGINED

WE CAN BUT TRY

PASS THE PUZZLE PARCEL
TOY TOMBOLA
LOUNGE MINI GOLF
HOOPLA
FISHING BINGO
CUP GAMES
MUSICAL LETTERS
THE RESTAURANT
PARTY GAMES
HOPSCOTCH
WHAT'S MISSING?
PAPER AEROPLANES
THE WASHING LINE
THE DETECTIVES
SHOVE PLATE-PENNY

WE CAN BUT TRY

It won't always work.

It feels strange to tell you this at the start of a book full of ideas, but I need to get it out there early doors. It just won't.

If having two children has taught me anything, it's that you need to set your expectations and assumptions at zero. That way, you're always pleasantly surprised!

As I've mentioned, the beauty of my 'it has to take no more than five minutes to set up' rule is that it doesn't matter if your little one ignores the game, or only plays for thirty seconds, or doesn't enjoy it, or (at worst) lobs it across the room. Since it only took you five minutes to set up, it's easy to just pop it all away again.

Sometimes your kiddy won't be in the mood. Sometimes the game you've chosen won't ignite their imagination. That's fine. You do you, kiddo.

If your child isn't interested in a game, you can:
- play the game yourself and see if that sparks their interest
- leave it out for later that day or for the next day, in case they change their mind
- put it away and try another time.

If your child changes the game while you're playing it, and they want to do it their own way, that's all good. Just go with it, and see where it takes you. If you're chatting together, you're doing already something great, no matter how the game is unfolding.

If your child decides halfway through the game that they don't want to play it any more, or if they start messing around to show their frustration, then just leave it. Walk away calmly. It doesn't matter one dot. If your kiddy doesn't want to play, then don't – the main aim is fun. If they aren't enjoying it, just stop.

I try to play one five-minute game for every morning or afternoon my kids and I are at home. The more you and your little folk play the games from this book together, the more you will get to know which ones are likely to be a big hit – the ones that will make their wee faces light up and make you feel like you're winning for a moment.

See, here's the thing: if you are *trying*, then you are brilliant. It is really all we can do, isn't it? Children are simply little humans who have their own very real emotions and moods. There are no guarantees as to what will work. It's all just trial and error – and the trial bit is what really matters, if you ask me.

So no, it won't always work. Give it a whirl anyway, because when your child loves it and you are both howling with laughter, as we all know, it can really feel quite magical.

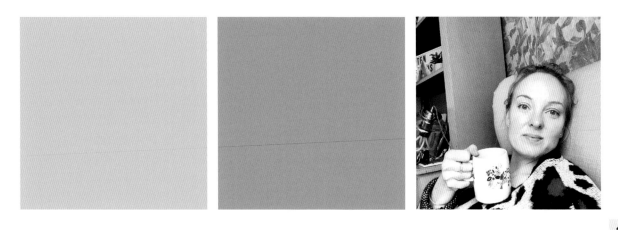

If it would usually be snack time after this game, you can pop the snack in the parcel as a surprise at the end!

If there's only you and one child, put out some teddies or dolls and let your child act on their behalf.

For older ones: Instead of using puzzle pieces, wrap letter blocks or magnets that spell out a word. (If you don't have any, write them on bits of paper and cut them out.) At the end, children have to solve the anagram.

PASS THE PUZZLE PARCEL

Puzzles. We've all got some, haven't we? You do them once, then they get thrown into a cupboard and are never, ever done again. So, let's use a party classic to jazz up a puzzle on a boring day at home! (And, by the way, if you do want your kids to play with a puzzle, lay it out for them to find. They won't pull it out themselves if it's in a box in the cupboard, but if it's all ready to go they'll more than likely give it a whirl – and you'll get five minutes of peace!)

GRAB:
- a puzzle
- some newspaper
- masking tape
- something to play music on

TO SET UP . . .
1. Spend five minutes wrapping the puzzle pieces in the newspaper, as you would for pass the parcel, putting one puzzle piece in each layer of the parcel.
2. Put some music on standby.
3. Leave the parcel out for your kids to find. **(REMEMBER THE GOLDEN RULE!)**

TO PLAY . . .
1. Sit in a circle, play the music and pass the parcel around.
2. Stop the music when no one is looking. The person holding the parcel when the music stops gets to open a layer.
3. They then put the puzzle piece in its correct place. Help them if they're having trouble or are really little.
4. Start the music again and repeat, letting children build the puzzle as they unwrap each piece!

When he was learning to count, Ewan kept missing out fifteen, so we played this game a lot to help!

For very little ones just learning numbers: Number the toys too. That way, they just need to match the toys and the tickets up.

TOY TOMBOLA

Just before Ewan started reception we were invited to his school's summer fair. I was so thrilled to discover that, in thirty years, absolutely nothing had changed! There were morris dancers, raffles and bouncy castles. The head teacher was cheerily making jokes on a dodgy tannoy that sporadically cut out. It all felt so familiar and comforting. I was especially delighted when we chanced upon the tombola stall – my childhood favourite was still firmly in place. Then I suddenly had a thought . . .

GRAB:

- a pen and some paper
- scissors
- a small box, basket or bag
- 5, 10 or 20 small toys (to match the number set up)

TO SET UP . . .

1. Write the numbers your child is learning (1–5, 1–10 or 1–20) on the paper, then cut out each number.
2. Fold the numbers up, and put them into the box, basket or bag.
3. Lay the small toys out in a line for your children to find.

TO PLAY . . .

1. Shake the box of numbers and say, **'ROLL UP! ROLL UP!'**
2. Ask children to choose a ticket and open it up. (Fiddly, but let them do it. Excellent fine motor skills!) Then ask them to say the number. (Help them if they're struggling.)
3. Once they know their number, count along the toy line together to find out which toy they've 'won'.
4. Remove the toy they've won, and replace it in the line with the number.
5. Repeat until all the toys have been won. By this point, your kids will have counted several times over and will also have a lovely number line to count along!

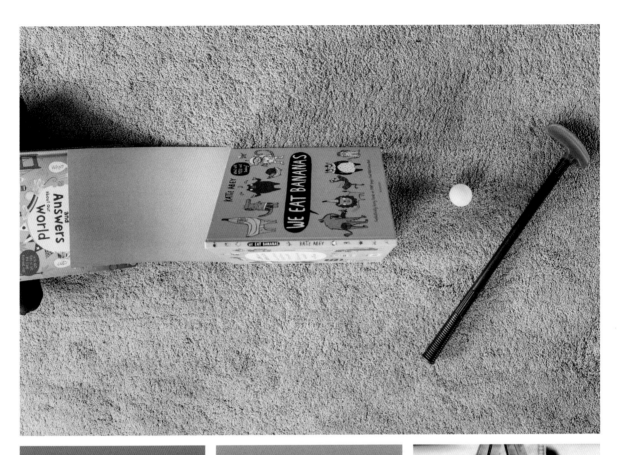

This is a great game for discussing the concepts of more and less with little ones.

LOUNGE MINI GOLF

You know when you get to the end of a roll of foil and there is always a piece that is stuck to it? Well, scrunch that bit of foil into a ball and keep the cardboard roll, and you've got two items for **MANY** games, including golf! We went to Center Parcs (out of school holidays – we aren't millionaires) when Ewan was nine months old. I casually handed the baby to his nanna and instantly hit a hole in one. I should have given up there and then, though, because I scored twenty-three on another hole trying to hit the damn ball through a tunnel!

GRAB:

- a cup
- loads of cushions
- a few large hardback books
- a small ball
- a tube or stick (something to use as a 'golf club')
- something to tally scores on

TO SET UP . . .

1. Tip the cup on its side to act as the 'hole', and put it where you want it.
2. Lay out a mini golf course using cushions.
3. You can use hardback books to make tunnels or ramps.
4. Put the ball and 'club' at the starting point, then wait for the kids to find it.

TO PLAY . . .

1. Show children how to play by giving them a quick demo.
2. One player hits their ball into the hole, while the other person records the number of shots on the score board.
3. Swap, so that each player has a turn hitting and a turn scoring.
4. The player with the lowest number of shots wins the hole.
5. Mix up the cushions, tunnels and hole, and play again!

I once used milk-bottle tops and wrote numbers on them for this game.

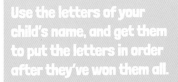

Use the letters of your child's name, and get them to put the letters in order after they've won them all.

HOOPLA

A funfair classic! Throw a hoop over something to win a prize! We play two versions of this game, one with big hula hoops in the garden and one with smaller hoops inside. When Halloween swings around, we often have loads of those little glow sticks knocking about the house – three sticks joined together with their little connectors make a perfect small hoop that you can reuse again and again.

GRAB:

- 5 cups
- 5 letters or numbers in any form (if you don't have any, write them on bits of paper and cut them out)
- a hoop

TO SET UP . . .

1. Pop the cups upside down, then put the letters or numbers on top of them. You can do this on the floor or along a low table or sofa at a child's waist height.
2. Leave the hoops nearby for the kids to find.

TO PLAY . . .

1. Let your little one try to win a letter or number by throwing the hoop over the cup.
2. You could also take it in turns, and the player with the most letters or numbers wins.

If your little one is struggling to recognize a certain letter, put that letter on their card alongside others that they know well.

FISHING BINGO

Yep, you read that correctly! Fishing. Bingo. Two activities usually enjoyed by the over-seventies reimagined for tiny folk. Who doesn't love a bit of bingo? Now, you can let your imagination run wild with this one and find all kinds of creative ways to pull the letter out of the 'hat'. No magnetic letters? We once wrote them on bits of paper, cut them out and used a straw to suck them out instead!

GRAB:

- a pen and some paper
- scissors
- magnetic letters
- something small and metal (a large paper clip, for example – we used a bottle opener out of a Christmas cracker!)
- a bit of string or ribbon
- a bowl

TO SET UP . . .

1. Use the pen and paper to make a bingo card for each player, with four of the available magnetic letters written on it. Each card should have a different set of letters for each player.
2. Tie the metal item to the string or ribbon. This is your 'fishing rod'.
3. Put the magnetic letters in the bowl, and follow the GOLDEN RULE.

TO PLAY . . .

1. Each player takes a bingo card. Then take it in turns to dip the 'fishing rod' into the bowl and fish out a magnetic letter.
2. If you have that letter on your bingo card, you get to take it and put it on top of your card.
3. The first player to get all four letters on their card and shout 'BINGO!' wins.

CUP GAMES

Sometimes, as a parent, you'll find yourself with a five-minute window while you wait for water to boil or the washing machine to finish its cycle. This is the best opportunity for a super-speedy game that gives your little ones a bit of attention without adding to your never-ending chores. And what do you need for these games? Cups!

CUP SKITTLES

GRAB:
- ■ 6 plastic or paper cups
- ■ a small football or tennis ball

TO SET UP . . .
1. Stack the cups into a pyramid on the floor, with three cups on the bottom, two on the next layer, and one on the top.

TO PLAY . . .
1. Kick the ball to knock the skittles over.
2. Take it in turns to stack the cups back up.
3. When you're done with kicking, you could try throwing or rolling the ball, or pushing it with your head, knee or elbow. Can your kids bounce it off the wall into the cups?

CUP COCONUT SHY

GRAB:
- 5 plastic or paper cups
- 5 toys, letters or numbers
- something to use as a marker on the floor, like a bit of string or a ruler
- a small football or tennis ball

TO SET UP . . .
1. Find a flat surface that's around kid height – two chairs side by side is a good option.
2. Put the cups upside down in a line, then pop one toy, letter or number on top of each cup.

TO PLAY . . .
1. Put a marker on the floor to show where to throw from.
2. Throw the ball at the cups to try to knock off the toys, letters or numbers.
3. Take turns to throw the ball, then set the cups and toys up again.

No cups? Use plastic bottles or bits and bobs out of the recycling bin.

If you want to make things more competitive, stop the music and shout out a letter for children to find – and race them to it!

MUSICAL LETTERS

In my experience, simple is always best. If my kids and I can play a game with just a pen and paper, it makes my day. No big clean-up and five minutes of feeling like I am nailing parenting because my kids have the biggest grins on their faces. Whenever I hear 'Can we play it again?' it's music to my ears! (Well not always, but, you know, if I'm in the mood for it!) And speaking of music . . .

GRAB:

- 10 bits of paper
- a pen
- something to play music on

TO SET UP . . .

1. On each piece of paper, write some letters. It could be the letters of your child's name or phonics sounds (see page 172 for more on phonics) or even words. I tend to mix it up, including a few letters my kids are confident with and a few that are new or that they get stuck on.
2. Spread the letters out on the floor.
3. Put the music on standby.

TO PLAY . . .

1. Explain to your little ones that, when the music plays, they can dance or run around between the letters. Then, when the music stops, they have to jump on a letter and shout it out. You jump on a letter too, and shout it out.
2. Remove the letters that get jumped on, then start the music again.
3. Keep going until there is only one letter left to win, or until all the letters are gone.

To extend play, children can wash up afterwards at the sink, using a bowl of soapy water and a cloth.

For older ones: Write the name of each item of food on the plates, instead of drawing them. You could even get children to write down the orders themselves!

2+

THE RESTAURANT

We have a basket of toy food that I think we probably play with every day. As thrilled as the kids enjoy it so much, sometimes when I'm eating plastic sausages and saying, 'Mmm delicious!' for the fifteenth time that day I want to swap lives with Daddy. So, I thought up a game that would make it a bit more interesting . . .

GRAB:

- a pen and some paper
- 5 plates or bowls
- toy food (if you don't have any, use small items of actual food from your cupboard)
- 5 soft toys

TO SET UP . . .

1. On a piece of paper, draw round a plate or bowl. Then trace or sketch three of the food items on to the plate. Finally draw one of the toys at the top of the page.
2. Repeat for each toy, using different food items for each. These are the toys' 'food orders'.
3. Set the toys out in a line or on a picnic blanket.
4. Leave the plates and toy food nearby, along with the orders.

TO PLAY . . .

1. Explain to your little ones that the toys have come to a restaurant, and that they have already placed their 'orders'.
2. Let your child select the toy they want to wait on and find its order.
3. Next, show your child how to search through the toy food to find the correct items to make up the order on a plate.
4. Finally they can take the meal they have made over to the toy.
5. Repeat with all the toys – and your children can 'feed' them their dinners at the end, if they want to!

Don't forget the good old classics too like musical bumps (sit down when the music stops) and musical statues (freeze when the music stops). Great for wearing them out. Pop on some tunes and have a five-minute boogie to finish your own little party!

PARTY GAMES

SPLAT THE RAT

You know when you finish a roll of wrapping paper and you feel like there is nothing more fun than bonking an unsuspecting person on the head with it? Well, there is something more fun you can do with it: save it for this little game (after you've bonked everyone on the head, of course!).

GRAB:

- masking tape
- a cardboard tube
- a cup
- something that will fit down the tube – a ball, a toy, or a bit of scrunched-up foil or paper

TO SET UP . . .

1. Tape the tube to a door or to the wall. Make sure it's at your child's height – they should be able to reach the top by stretching their arm.
2. Put the cup and the ball or toy on the floor nearby.

TO PLAY . . .

1. Explain to your kids that they have to drop the ball or toy down the tube and catch it in the cup. They can hold the cup or put the cup on the floor, under the tube.
2. When they can do this easily, get them to see if they can catch the ball or toy in their hands.
3. Once they've mastered this, they can use a 'bat' (like another cardboard tube or their hand) to splat it – or, in other words, to hit it with before it touches the ground.

You could also do this for a version of Silly Soup (see page 169). While blindfolded, children select two consonants and one vowel, then remove the blindfold to see the silly word they've created.

2+

PIN THE FEATURES ON THE FACE

The main reason I invented this game is because I can't for the life of me draw a flipping donkey! But I can draw a face. It's amazing what being trapped at home with two kids on a rainy November day does to my imagination – anything to stop the whinge!

GRAB:

- a pen and some paper or card
- scissors
- Blu-Tack (if you don't have any, play dough will do)
- something to use as a blindfold

TO SET UP . . .

1. Draw three quick faces with different features, for example, one wide nose, one pointy nose, etc. on the paper or card.
2. Cut out each feature, then stick a bit of Blu-Tack to the back.
3. Draw an oval face shape on to a big piece of paper, then tack it to the wall or a window.
4. Place the cut-out features above the oval face shape.
5. Put the blindfold nearby.

TO PLAY . . .

1. When your little ones find this set-up, show them how to put the blindfold on.
2. Explain that, while blindfolded, they have to pick one of the features and try to stick it in the right place on the face, and keep going until they've made a face. You can talk to them about the feature they've selected, and gently guide them towards the right spot.
3. Once they've made their funny face, let them take off the blindfold for a giggle.

Depending on your indoor floor surfaces, you might be able to chalk out a hopscotch inside or use number mats! Use blobs of Blu-Tack or play dough instead of stones.

HOPSCOTCH

Now, I obviously didn't invent hopscotch, but I do feel like this long-lost game needs to be brought back. I used to play it with my nan all the time. She would chalk out the hopscotch on the path in front of her house and we'd spend a good ten minutes playing. I'm not sure whether these are the official rules, but it's how my nan and I played and it was always fun.

GRAB:

- some chalk
- some stones

TO SET UP . . .

1. Draw out the hopscotch on the ground.
2. Leave the stones nearby.

TO PLAY . . .

1. Take it in turns to stand in front of the first square, then throw your stone. The idea is to land the stone on each number consecutively – so, to start with, you're aiming for 1, then 2, and so on.
2. When your stone lands on the right number, you hop through the hopscotch WITHOUT putting your foot on the number where your stone is. If you wobble and put your foot down on it, then you have to do that number again.
3. Once you have completed the hopscotch without landing on the number where your stone is, you can move on to the next number.
4. The winner is the first person to get to 10.

Extend the game by letting your child choose five items, then you guess what's missing.

2+

WHAT'S MISSING?

This lovely five-minute game is perfect for little ones who are developing their speech and language. I was reminded of it on a training course, and when I took it back into the classroom the kids loved it. I was prompted to play it again when Ewan was struggling to pronounce his Fs, and I needed something that would encourage him to practise the sound without realizing it.

GRAB:

- 5 small items (for Ewan, I used things that all began with F – fork, the number 5, fire engine, etc. – but you can use any small items if you don't need to focus on a particular letter sound)
- a tray
- a tea towel

TO SET UP . . .

1. Pop the items on the tray, then cover it with a tea towel.
2. Leave it in a place where your child will discover it.

TO PLAY . . .

1. Once your child has found the tray, lift the tea towel to reveal the items underneath. Can they name all the items?
2. Now ask them to close their eyes, then remove one item from the tray and put the tea towel back over it.
3. Ask them to open their eyes, then lift up the tea towel. Can they work out which item you've removed? If they need to jog their memory, you can name them all again together.
4. Once they've figured out which item is missing, repeat, removing a different item each time.

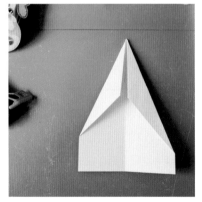

Leave out some extra paper or card so that your kids can have a go at making their own aeroplanes.

Experiment with adding paper clips or masking tape to various parts of the aeroplanes. Does this make them fly better?

PAPER AEROPLANES

A true classic! We've all done this one as kids, haven't we? If you don't already have a preferred folding technique, here are pictures of mine on the page opposite. I like to use thin card, as it makes the aeroplanes sturdier. You could actually use aeroplanes in place of balls for a lot of the games in this chapter – for example, Cup Skittles (see page 24) could be knocked over with a decent paper aeroplane, if you fancy. Here are two of our favourite paper-aeroplane games.

GRAB:

- some thin card or paper
- some pens
- scissors

TO SET UP (GAME 1) . . .

1. Make one paper aeroplane per player, with my folding technique or your own.
2. On bits of card or paper, write down some letters or numbers, and cut them out.
3. Fold the bits of card so each letter or number stands up on its own.
4. On a footstool or a coffee table, line up the letters or numbers. These are your 'targets'.

TO SET UP (GAME 2) . . .

1. Make one paper aeroplane per player, with my folding technique or your own.
2. On bits of card, write large numbers or letters. These are your 'airports'.
3. Place the airports around the room on sofas or on the floor.

TO PLAY . . .

1. Each player takes turns throwing their aeroplane to knock down the targets or attempt to land at the airports.

An easy version is using masking tape as a sticky line but it doesn't have the same hanging effect.

For very little ones: If younger children want to join in with older siblings, just put out some old cloths or socks and let them hang out the washing too!

THE WASHING LINE

This game was born during a glorious summer heatwave. We'd spent the long, hot days running around the garden – my favourite play space – but we hadn't done much letter recognition, as I'd been busy blowing up paddling pools and slapping factor fifty on my wriggly toddlers. While I sat watching my washing get bleached by the sun, an idea popped into my head. I set off to the shed to rummage around for the things I needed to set up a game that would justify an ice cream for all of us afterwards!

GRAB:

- a long piece of string
- something to use as two 'posts' – I used chairs, but you could use garden canes, trees, anything at all
- a pen and some paper (I used Post-its)
- scissors (if you don't have Post-its)
- some pegs

TO SET UP . . .

1. Make your 'washing line' by tying the string between the two posts.
2. Write each letter of your child's name on paper or on individual Post-its. If using paper, cut out each letter. I wrote Ewan's full name to introduce more letters, but do whatever your child can confidently manage.
3. Jumble up the letters and put them on the floor or the ground next to the washing line with the pegs.

TO PLAY . . .

1. Explain that all your child has to do is hang up the letters of their name in the right order, using the pegs. You can help them to find the right letters as much or as little as they need. Ask, 'What comes next?'
2. Using pegs is a great way to build muscle strength in little hands, and uses the same muscles needed for writing!
3. If the bits of paper spin round, you might need to put a peg on the bottom. If you're using Post-its, you can peg them with the peg pointing up and the Post-it clipped above the line (like I've done in the bottom left picture on the opposite page).

It's your turn to be the detective! When your kids have rescued their toy, let them have a turn hiding it and making clues for you to find it.

If you want to get your kids moving, make sure the clues take them upstairs and downstairs and back again. This will also make the game last longer!

You can obviously add as many clues as you like. Fancy a cuppa in peace? Do 15 cryptic clues!

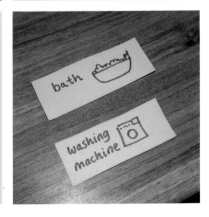

3+

abc

1²3

THE DETECTIVES

I played this as a kid, and I can vaguely remember hiding clues around the house for friends who came over after school for 'tea' (always fish fingers, chips and beans – happy days). It's the sort of game my friend Sarah and I would play with our favourite toy hedgehogs, while her little sister Alice tried to muscle in on the action with her third-wheel hedgehog. If we were feeling generous, we'd let Alice play too. So, in tribute to them both, I've made up a version that everyone can join in with!

GRAB:

- a soft toy
- child-friendly scissors
- a pen and some paper
- a magnifying glass (optional)

TO SET UP . . .

1. Hide the soft toy somewhere in the house. You can get inventive and tie it up on a curtain rail or similar . . . or else you can just stuff it behind the TV like I did!
2. Cut out five bits of paper, then number them 1 to 5 with the pen. Flip each card over, and write or draw a clue for where the next clue will be. So, card 1 has a clue for where card 2 is, and so on. On card 5, write or draw a clue for where the toy is hiding. If your child is only wee, draw pictures as clues – the bath, the washing machine, the garden, etc. If they are just learning to read, perhaps draw a picture and write the word. If they are older and you want to encourage them to read, just write the clue.
3. Pop the first clue by the front door with the magnifying glass (if using) and a note that says: 'The toy has been held hostage!'
4. Hide the rest of the clues in the correct places around the house.

TO PLAY . . .

1. When your kids spot the note and clue by the front door, read them together. Say, 'Oh no! We have to save your toy! You are the detective, and you must figure out the clues!'
2. Then help them to figure out the first clue. Ask, 'What number comes next? Where could it be?' When they work it out, send them on their way.
3. Let them try to figure out the rest of the clues on their own, running all over the house. Littler ones may need some support – when I did this with my two, I made a different set of clues for each of them, then stuck with Flo while Ewan worked his clues out by himself.
4. Finally free the toy! Hurrah!

You can take it in turns to shove, if you want, but I just let the kids shove at the same time. It's chaos, but brilliant fun!

SHOVE PLATE-PENNY

When my grandma was cleaning out her house to move, the only thing my mum and dad requested was the family Shove Ha'penny board, because they had played it over and over as teenage sweethearts. They still have that board now. Shove Ha'penny is a brilliant game, and my family has spent many an evening playing it together and winding each other up. To play, you shove a ha'penny across the board, trying to get it to land perfectly in the number lines. So I came up with this version. If my brother is reading this, I bagsy the board!

GRAB:

- masking tape
- some chalk
- a pen and some paper
- a plastic plate or Frisbee for each player

TO SET UP . . .

1. Use the masking tape to make six horizontal lines on a smooth, hard floor. The lines should be far enough apart that the plate or Frisbee can sit between them with a few centimetres of space either side. These are your tramlines.
2. Within each tramline on one side, write something in chalk that you would like your little one to learn – numbers, shapes, letters, words, spellings or whatever you wish. When I played with my two, I did numbers 1 to 5 for Flo and tricky words for Ewan. If chalk doesn't work on your floor, just write on bits of paper instead.
3. Write each child's name on a bit of paper – this is their scorecard. If your little one can't write yet, also write the things that are between their tramlines, so they can just circle them or tick them off.

TO PLAY . . .

1. Explain to your little ones that each player has to shove their plate across the room so that it lands perfectly between the tramlines without touching them.
2. When a player gets their plate to land within a set of tramlines, they get whatever is written there. They must then write down that thing on their scorecard (or tick it off, if they are too little to write it).
3. The winner is the first player to get all five.
4. Keep shoving until everyone has got all five, then rub out the chalk, write something new in the tramlines and play again!

FIVE TIPS FOR ENCOURAGING SPEECH AND LANGUAGE

Like everything when it comes to a child's development, there is a large window for when speech will start and the speed at which it'll develop. Every child does things at their own pace, but we've all got that friend who just loves to tell us how advanced their little Jonny is. 'He's already counting to ten in Mandarin! The other night he asked to read *War and Peace* for his goodnight story!'

However, if you are at all worried about your little one's speech development, don't hesitate to discuss it with your family doctor, your health visitor, or your child's nursery assistant or teacher. These professionals can give you advice on engaging a speech and language therapist, if additional support is required.

If you are keen to support your child with speech and language at home, playing five-minute games is always a good thing to do. When I was a teaching assistant, I was trained in how to support children with speech and language difficulties. So, although I am not a speech and language therapist, I have designed all my games to help your little ones practise language learning at home in a really easy FIVE MINUTE WAY!

Here are five easy things that I do to help my little ones with their speech:

1. THE PAUSE

Reading books together is one of the best ways to help with speech development. A great way to encourage your kids to chatter is to use 'the pause'. All you do is get a book you read regularly that has a rhyming story. Then, when you get to the end of a line, pause. Let your child try to finish the sentence. You can point to clues in the pictures to help them.

2. SLOUCHED–DOWN SINGING

Spend five minutes a day singing nursery rhymes with your little one. Sit them on your belly, then slouch right down on the sofa so that they can see your lips move as you make the words. This little thing can have a huge impact.

3. MAKE EYE CONTACT

Play down at your child's level. When you're playing cars or dolls or doctors and nurses – whatever your child loves most – lie on your tummy and get yourself down there with them!

4. MODEL

If your child says something incorrectly, just repeat it back to them in the correct form. This way, you show them how it should sound without battering their precious confidence. For example, if your child tells you, 'I runneded to the swide!' simply reply, 'Yes, I saw you run to the slide. You're so fast!' Sounds obvious – and it is – but often, as parents, we just need a nudge on the simplest of things, don't we? I know I do.

5. CHATTER AWAY!

Talk to your little one about what you are doing as you get ready for work, unload the dishwasher, make the bed, get them dressed. Describe the things you see when you are out and about with them. Chat, chat, chat! Easy and effective.

INTRODUCING LETTERS AND NUMBERS

STEALTH LEARNING

ALPHABET CAR PARK
BOOK DETECTIVE
THE MAGIC CUP
LETTER SPINNER
TREASURE HUNT
TARGET PRACTICE
THE ALPHABET TRAIN
THE BALL PIT
THE HUNGRY PUPPET
RUB IT OUT
A SPOONFUL OF SUGAR
LETTER RACETRACK
THE TRAP
POP!
NUMBER JUMP
LETTER QUARRY
MATCHING GAMES
LETTER OF THE DAY

STEALTH LEARNING

There comes a point when looking after children at which you've done the bum-wiping and the burping and you think, **WHAT NEXT?** You want your kids to learn useful things, like what their own name looks like written down, but you don't necessarily want them to **KNOW** they are learning, because if you've ever tried to tell a three-year-old what to do you'll know **ANY** idea you've suggested (like perhaps getting dressed or eating anything other than chips) is treated like you've asked Beyoncé to do the summer season at Butlins.

But who can blame them? When it comes to fun, nothing, in my opinion, is more of a turn-off than the word 'educational'. This goes for adults as well as for kids. I've never been on one of those training courses and thought, **HURRAH, IT'S EDUCATIONAL FUN TODAY!** What I would prefer is a day of pure pleasure (drinking cocktails on a sun lounger, please) with the learning part added in by stealth ('If you can tell me what eight times six is, Daisy, you win ten extra minutes lounging in the sun!'). My kids are just the same.

So, let's get sneaky! Folks often ask me how to get their little ones to engage with learning, and my reply is always, 'What is their favourite thing to do?' If you know this, then that's all you need. Find a way to incorporate the learning bit into the fun bit. In this chapter, I've covered all sorts of ways to do this, but you can easily invent your own activities when you've got the idea. It's easy once you get into the swing of it. Just set your dial to sleuth mode.

You might be wondering what is a good age to start number and letter recognition with your children. My reply is: start from day one. I'm not suggesting that the second you set eyes on your tiny human you should shout, 'Hey, baby! Your name begins with E!' What I mean is that numbers and letters should just be a part of their world. Chances are, they already are – even if you don't realize it. When you read books to your children, you are starting the process. When you count as you go up the stairs, you are doing it. When you sing nursery rhymes like 'Five Currant Buns', you are being a **FREAKING AWESOME PARENT**.

If these sorts of things are an everyday part of your child's little world, then you'll spot when they naturally take more of an interest. When they ask, 'What does that sign say?' or 'How many is this?' **THAT'S YOUR CUE** to try the games in this chapter. This can start at any age, but for me it was when my kids turned three that it seemed the most natural time to try out these games and see what sparked their excitement. It took Ewan until he was four to really get to grips with his letters, but for Flo it's been earlier, although numbers seem to pass her by. Each child does everything in their own time. Competitive parenting is futile – no adult boasts that they could use scissors at three years old! As always, be led by them.

I hope there is something for everyone in this chapter. These are games that were inspired by my own children and by other kids I know. There are games for little ones who are happier sitting quietly looking at stories, and games for the type who simply adore chucking stuff and making as much noise as humanly possible. We are all different, and so our ways of learning should be too.

Make it even more exciting by adding a ramp or by using masking tape to make a road to the car park!

You could combine this with Letter Racetrack on page 75.

ALPHABET CAR PARK

There was a time when Ewan was only interested in vehicles. If it had wheels, he was up for it. If it didn't, then he wasn't bothering. At home we had trains, trucks, diggers, tractors and cars coming out of our ears, yet whenever we went to playgroup he'd bolt for the train track and the corner with the cars. What's that about? I've paid £2.50 for this, mate, why not try out a doll? So, to spark an interest in the alphabet, I realized I needed to find a way to get transportation fun and letters to collide.

GRAB:

- a bit of cardboard (a flattened-out cereal box is ideal)
- a pen
- around 5 toy cars

TO SET UP . . .

1. Draw a rectangular grid that's five rectangles across the top and six down on the cardboard. Each rectangle needs to be big enough to fit a toy car, and you'll end up with thirty rectangles.
2. Write a letter of the alphabet in each rectangle. You can write the letters in alphabetical or a random order, leaving four blank spaces around the grid.
3. Pop any toy cars you have next to the cardboard grid, and follow the GOLDEN RULE.

TO PLAY . . .

1. Explain to your little one that they need to park the cars in their spaces. Demonstrate how to do this by saying, for example, 'I'm going to park this blue car in this spot with "r" in it.' Then park the car in the correct spot.
2. Now let your child park the cars. If they don't say the letter of the space they park in, that doesn't matter – just say something like, 'You parked that car on "f".' Ask them questions like, 'Where's the green car going to park?'
3. See if they can find the letters of their name to park on.

If your kids are confident writers, get them to write down five letters they can see on the books for you to find.

Make your own 'magnifying glass' by cutting one out of cardboard.

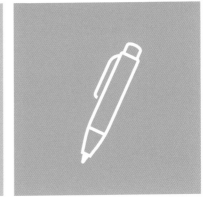

BOOK DETECTIVE

One sunny day, after I had managed to get Flo to nap in her cot (hurrah, I won!), I wanted five minutes of quiet time. So I set up this game for Ewan under a big umbrella in the garden. We had an ice lolly as we played, then I used the rest of Florence's nap time to bask in the sunshine guilt-free. Some days I feel like being a stay-at-home mum is too damn hard, and then there are moments like these when I think it's the best job in the world.

GRAB:

- 6 books
- a pen and some paper
- a magnifying glass (optional)

TO SET UP . . .

1. Lay the books out on the ground so you can see the front covers clearly.
2. Write six letters on the paper that you can see on the covers of the books. Next to each letter draw a small tick box.
3. If you have a magnifying glass, leave it beside the books and the letters.

TO PLAY . . .

1. Explain to your kids that they have to find each of the letters you have written down on the paper by searching the covers of the books, using the magnifying glass (if you have one). Let them choose which letter they want to look for first.
2. Once they've found a match, put a little tick in the box next to that letter.
3. Once they have found all the letters, see if they want to do it again. If they do, turn over the bits of paper and write down a new set of letters. If not, choose a book to read together.

If you can move fast enough, swap the letter for a small toy and watch your child lose their tiny mind!

2+

abc

THE MAGIC CUP

This one is inspired by Ewan and Florence's grandad. He absolutely loves to do magic tricks on the kids, who are always thrilled and mystified by them. He knows he only has a short window of them believing he can do magic, so he's going for gold with it! Florence once tried to copy his trick of throwing a toy car into the trees, then magically producing it from behind his back – but she actually lobbed the car, which promptly smashed into smithereens. She looked flabbergasted and declared wide-eyed, 'I can't do it!' I'm sure one day Grandad will share his magic secrets with her, but for now we'll all just pretend we're as surprised as she is.

GRAB:

- 3 matching cups that you can't see through
- 5 plastic or magnetic letters – if you don't have any, write some on paper and cut them out

TO SET UP . . .

1. Pop the cups upside down in a line near the edge of a table you can sit at.
2. Put five letters out next to them.

TO PLAY . . .

1. Ask your little one to choose a letter and pop it under one of the cups.
2. Whizz the cups around, mixing up the order.
3. Ask your child to tell you which cup they think the letter is under. Look under the cup. If the letter isn't there, let them choose another one. When they do find the letter, celebrate with them and put that letter in a pile next to them.
4. Now choose another letter and hide it under another cup.
5. Whizz the cups around again, but this time let the letter discreetly fall out and on to your lap without your child seeing it. Hide the letter in your hand.
6. Ask your child to guess which cup the letter is under. When they can't find it, pretend to pull it from behind their ear. MAGIC!
7. Repeat using all five of the letters. Each time, 'find' the letter in a different place – under your chair, on the table, or even (if you can distract them!) pop it under a different cup.

Write numbers on your spinner and use it instead of a dice for other games.

LETTER SPINNER

Despite how it might appear, I am not a 'crafty' mamma. Folks who do crafty things with little ones are all sorts of wonderful, but this here game is about as crafty as I get. The reason I don't do much crafting with my kids is simply because I find that the greater the amount of time I spend setting up (and cleaning up) an activity, the less time my kids spend actually doing the flippin' thing. Anyone else find this? As I ask through gritted teeth, 'Are you really finished, darling? Are you **SURE** you don't want to do any more sequin sticking?' I can feel the rage exploding in my brain. So, here's how I get crafty – **FIVE MINUTE STYLE**.

GRAB:

- a ruler
- a bit of cardboard for each player
- some felt-tip pens
- scissors (and child-friendly scissors if your child can cut out their own spinner)
- a sharp pencil
- some paper

TO SET UP . . .

1. Use the ruler and a pen to draw a hexagon on a bit of cardboard. (A hexagon has six sides. Don't worry, I had to double-check too!)
2. Draw a line to the centre of the hexagon from each corner. This will create six triangles inside the hexagon.
3. In each triangle, write a letter.
4. Depending on what each player is capable of, either draw another hexagon containing letters on to a bit of cardboard for them or draw one using dotted lines that they can trace over. You could also just leave a blank bit of cardboard out for them to copy their own hexagon on to.
5. Cut out your hexagon, then push a sharp pencil through the centre of it so that the hexagon spins on the pencil. This is your 'letter spinner'.
6. Write the letters that are in your hexagon on a bit of paper, then put a tick box next to each letter. Do this for each player.

TO PLAY . . .

1. Show children your letter spinner, then support them to make their own. If necessary, help them with writing, cutting and putting the pencil through the centre.
2. Once your spinners are made, take turns to spin them.
3. On your list, tick off each letter when you land on it (the side with the triangle touching the floor).
4. The first player to tick off all their letters wins!

TREASURE HUNT

This was one of the first ideas I ever had and shared on my blog. It started with a wooden puzzle board – the kind with lots of shapes or objects, and kids have to slot the correct piece into the correct hole. Brilliant for those very early fine motor skills and for speech. (Plus, watching chubby little hands try to bash the pieces into the slots is super cute.) But what about when your kids can confidently do this sort of puzzle? Do you just hand it on? Hold your horses! You might just get a bit more use out of it yet.

GRAB:

- a puzzle board
- *or* some small toys, a pen and some paper if you don't have a puzzle board

TO SET UP . . .

1. If you don't have a puzzle board, use the pen to trace the shape of the toys on to the piece of paper.
2. Hide the puzzle pieces or the toys around a room.
3. Leave the empty puzzle board or piece of paper in full view.

TO PLAY . . .

1. Explain to your children that they have to search the room to find all the missing pieces – and they have to do it as fast as they can!

VARIATIONS

Yes, it's really that easy! Here are some more ideas for adding letters and numbers:
1. Use a puzzle board where the puzzle is either the letters of the alphabet or numbers.
2. You can still use letters and numbers even if you only have a picture puzzle board. Simply write down the letters that correspond to the pictures on a bit of paper, so if you have a car, house and ball, for example, you write c, h and b. Cut them out so they fit in the empty puzzle slots when the pieces are taken out. Then, when your child finds the house puzzle piece, you can say, 'Which letter must it be?' And look for the letter h on the board, as well as the matching shape, to return the puzzle piece to its correct slot.
3. Likewise with numbers, cut out individual numbers that equal the number of puzzle pieces you have on your board, then pop them into the empty slots. When your child finds a puzzle piece, you can say, 'You found number 4, a car,' for example. You can see which numbers you still have left to find when they are on the last ones: 'We still need number 8 – I wonder what that could be?'

You can play this game and its variations with numbers instead of letters!

There are endless ways to play this game! Just follow your little one's interests and go with what you think they will love.

TARGET PRACTICE

One day when Ewan was three and I was tired of playing the same old games with him, I wrote E, W, A and N on four wallpaper scraps and hung them out on our washing line. Then I gave Ewan his foam rocket launcher and asked if he wanted to see something cool. He ran towards the letters and shot them, laughing and completely oblivious (or so I thought) to me shouting, 'You hit the E for your name!' and 'Yay! You got the A!' Then about a month later he painted a perfect E. 'Mummy,' he declared, 'that's E for Ewan.' My heart exploded with joy. So, if you've been wondering whether five minutes is enough, it really is.

GRAB:

- anything you can write the letters of your child's name on
- something to throw or launch, such as a small ball, a beanbag, sponge or paper plane

TO SET UP . . .

1. Put the letters somewhere outside where there's plenty of room – on a washing line, pinned to trees or tacked to walls or sheds.
2. Leave the item to throw or launch nearby.

TO PLAY . . .

1. Explain to your little ones that the aim is to hit the letters. As they hit each letter, shout it out!
2. Can they hit the letters in order to spell out their name?

VARIATIONS

Here are some other versions of this game that I've played with my two:
1. Chalk letters on to a wall or the floor and throw wet sponges. **SPLAT!**
2. Stick paper letters to a fence and throw foam rockets with a blob of paint on the end.
3. Write letters in the sand at the beach and throw stones.
4. Write letters on to bits of cardboard that you fold over and stand on the ground, then kick a football at them.
5. Stick letters on cups turned upside down and lined up on a shelf, then use a ball to knock them off.

To get your child's interest, start by leaving passengers on the letters of their name.

THE ALPHABET TRAIN

All aboard! When Ewan was wee, he was obsessed with *Thomas & Friends*. My husband and I can still sing every word of the theme song. (And they say kids kill the romance, eh?) Anyway, my point is that pairing up locomotives and letters was the perfect way to wedge a bit of learning into our playtime. So, who else has had a dinner conversation about how useful an engine Thomas really is, even when the kids aren't around?

GRAB:

- A to Z foam letter tiles that connect together (if you don't have any, write letters on paper)
- 5 soft toys
- a small cart or wagon if you have one (optional)

TO SET UP . . .

1. Make an alphabet track through your house by connecting the foam letter tiles or by writing the alphabet on bits of paper. This is your 'train track'.
2. Put the five soft toys on five different letters. These are your 'passengers'.
3. Leave the cart or wagon at the start of the track (if you're using it).

TO PLAY . . .

1. Explain to your little one that they are the train, and the cart is their carriage (if using). The 'train' has to travel along the train tracks – saying, 'Choo-choo!' – and stop at each station where a passenger is waiting.
2. When they stop, say the letter of the station. For example, say, 'You've stopped at Station F! All aboard!' Then the train picks up the passenger and moves on to the next one.
3. Once they have collected all the passengers, let your child put the passengers at different stations and it's your turn to be the train! Remember to say each of the letters as you **CHUGGER–CHUGGER** your way down the tracks.

If using a paddling pool, fill it with water and use a sieve to fish out the balls. Don't forget to keep an eye on your little ones when they play with water!

For little ones who are just learning their letters: Write the letters of their name on bits of paper and pop them in the muffin tray, to be matched with the letters on the balls.

For very little ones: Ask them to find balls of a particular colour, and throw away the rest.

For older ones: Put random letters on lots of balls, then ask them to use the balls to see what words they can make!

THE BALL PIT

Don't worry, this game has nothing to do with the horror that is a soft-play ball pit – or the things you'll find at the bottom of them! Lots of parents I know have at some point or another bought a big bag of balls. These are particularly useful if you feel as though you don't already tidy up enough, and would like to scoop endless balls out from underneath your sofa and sideboard for extra fun. Usually the 'ball bag of regret' ends up hidden in the depths of the 'stuff we never play with' cupboard . . . but ah-ha! I have found a use for it!

GRAB:

- a bag of balls
- something big enough to put all the balls in (for example, an empty paddling pool, a big bowl or a bucket)
- a marker pen
- a pen and some paper
- a muffin tray, or paper or plastic cups

TO SET UP . . .

1. Pop all the balls into whatever receptacle you have.
2. Use the marker pen to write each letter of your little one's name on to individual balls. Depending on how confident they are, you can just do their first name or their full name.
3. Leave the muffin tray somewhere nearby.

TO PLAY . . .

1. Explain to your children that they have to search through the balls to find the ones with the letters of their name on them.
2. As they search, get them to pull one ball out at a time. If a ball doesn't have a letter on it, shout, 'Throw it away!' and let your child chuck it. If a ball does have a letter, get them to pop it in the muffin tray or cups in the correct order to spell out their name.

The more confident children are, the more letters you can use. Just make sure there are always letters they know well in the mix.

3+

abc

THE HUNGRY PUPPET

The sillier you are when playing these games, the more your kids will enjoy it! If you pretend to get it wrong, make funny voices and just generally appeal to their sense of humour, the laughter will follow. The top priority for all my five-minute games is always fun. First and foremost, it should be a joy to play – and anything else is a bonus. This game gives you lots of opportunities to be very, very silly, and in this very serious world I think we could all do with five minutes of silliness!

GRAB:

- a large old sock or oven glove, or a hand puppet
- some stick-on googly eyes (optional) or a marker pen
- a pen and some paper
- scissors

TO SET UP . . .

1. Turn the old sock or glove into a puppet by adding googly eyes (or by drawing some on) and a tongue. If you have a hand puppet, you can just use that.
2. Write each letter from your child's name on a bit of paper, then cut each letter out individually.

TO PLAY . . .

1. Introduce your puppet. Give it a silly name, and make it speak by opening and closing its mouth. Tell your little ones that it is **VERY** hungry and enjoys lots of snacks. Say, 'To start with, it would like a . . . G!' (But you can say any letter, obviously!)
2. Children then have to feed the puppet the correct letter. When they get it right, the puppet says, 'Yum! Yum!' If they get it wrong, the puppet says, 'Yuck! Yuck!' and spits it back out again.
3. Keep going until all the letters are eaten. The naughty puppet saves a big burp for the very end, when it spits all the letters out on the kids' heads!
4. Now let your kids have a turn at being the puppet.

RUB IT OUT

As you know, one of my rules is that any game needs to be just as quick to clean up as it is to set up. Well, in this one the cleaning up is the game. A win-win, as it's never too early to introduce the idea of tidying up! This game is great because it's a really easy and fun way to get your kids to engage with reading without even realizing it.

GRAB:

- anything that you can draw with and also wipe out – chalk, a whiteboard pen, chalk/paint sticks, shaving foam
- something to wipe out – wet wipes, kitchen paper, water and a cloth, a clean paintbrush

TO SET UP . . .

1. Write your child's name, or a selection of letters or numbers.
2. Leave the items for cleaning up nearby.

TO PLAY . . .

1. Explain to your kids that they have to rub out the things that you write.
2. You can race against the clock or just shout out the letters or numbers you want them to erase.

VARIATIONS

Here are some other versions of this game that I've played with my two:

1. My kids try to beat me by making the letters or numbers disappear as quickly as I can write them.
2. I write on the floor with chalk, and the kids 'paint' it off with water. (They can use a chunky paintbrush, or just their hands!)
3. I write on a low window or door with a whiteboard marker, and the kids wipe it off with kitchen paper.
4. I write in sand with a stick, and the kids rub it out with their feet or hands.
5. I use a paint stick on a patio door, and the kids wipe it out with wet wipes.
6. I write with shaving foam on a tiled bathroom wall or shower screen, and the kids clean with a facecloth.

If you use cornflour as a substitute for the 'sugar', it'll make gloop tea, which is always fun to touch and play with afterwards!

This one can get messy, so perhaps put down a mat or old towel!

2+

A SPOONFUL OF SUGAR

Florence loves making cups of tea. She has a large collection of tea sets all over the house, because if I get one out it's guaranteed that she'll happily sit for a good ten minutes of solitary engaged play. Heaven! So, just like Ewan with his trains, I wanted to find a way we could enjoy Flo's favourite toy together and perhaps learn a few numbers to boot.

GRAB:

- 4 bits of paper
- a pen
- 4 soft toys
- a tea set (if you don't have one, use a small jug and bowl, plastic cups and teaspoons)
- a tray
- some water
- a bag of flour

TO SET UP . . .

1. On four separate bits of paper, draw a cup and a number between 1 and 4. These are your 'orders'.
2. Set the four soft toys up for a tea party around the tea set on the tray.
3. Pop an 'order' next to each soft toy.
4. Fill the teapot with water.
5. Put some flour in a 'sugar' bowl.

TO PLAY . . .

1. Explain that the toys have come to have a tea party. Show children the toys' orders.
2. Get your child to choose a toy and its order. Then show them how to pour the water and add the number of spoonfuls of sugar the toy has ordered. (This is the number on the toy's 'order'.) Carefully count out each spoonful together.
3. Once your child has made the tea and added the correct number of sugars, they give it to the toy. 'Ah, lovely! Thank you!' says the toy.
4. Repeat for all the toys and their 'orders'.

If you don't have a box, an old wallpaper roll works well. Single rolls can be bought very cheaply in DIY shops.

1+

LETTER RACETRACK

Giant cardboard boxes are the best. You can quite literally throw one in the direction of your kids and go and make a cup of tea. Just like bubbles, kids go freaking nuts for a big old box. And, once they've run out of things to do with it, cut it down and lay it out flat and you've got yourself an instant racetrack!

GRAB:

- a large cardboard box
- a pen
- a toy car for each player

TO SET UP . . .

1. Write your child's name in the style of a road along the flattened-out box.
2. If you like, you can add an Alphabet Car Park (see page 53) at one end.
3. Leave the cars nearby.

TO PLAY . . .

1. Each player chooses a car and drives it along the letter roads. Tell your little one the letters you are driving along. See if they want to join in.
2. If you have an Alphabet Car Park at the end of the racetrack, park the cars in it.
3. You could also write your name alongside your child's and have a race!
4. Or perhaps try taping a pen to the back of your child's car, then see if they can draw around the racetrack with it.

To make it trickier, choose two 'traps'!

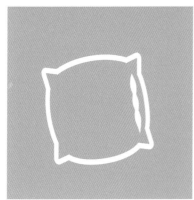

If your kids know the story of the Three Billy Goats Gruff, play with a troll instead of a croc!

THE TRAP

Good for a rainy day, this one. Invented in my living room one drizzly May afternoon, in a fit of 'Right, the telly is going off now!' then a sudden panic of 'Oh crikey, now what shall we do?' As usual, I looked around me for inspiration. Something that doesn't require my lazy bum to actually do much is always ideal. And what did I spot? Cushions. Now, we'd just been watching **PETER PAN**, and the crocodile is very much a favourite character. How about the hungry croc comes to play?

GRAB:

- 5 small cushions
- a pen and some paper

TO SET UP . . .

1. Put the cushions in a line across a room between one sofa or chair and another – this is your 'bridge', and the floor is the 'water'.
2. Write anything you want your little one to learn on five bits of paper – it could be the letters of their name, numbers, words or phonics (see page 172). Anything! Write a set of five for each player.
3. Pop a bit of paper on each cushion.

TO PLAY . . .

1. Each player takes it in turns to try to cross the cushion bridge. But before they start to cross, you tell them that one of the cushions is a trap!
2. Say, 'The one with the trap has a . . .' and then you choose one of the words, letters or numbers that is on the trap cushion. So, for example, with Ewan I might say, 'The word "the" is the trap.'
3. Help the player to read all the words on the cushions in order to find the trap one. Once they spot which one it is, they can then cross the bridge, being careful to jump over the trap cushion with the trap word on it.
4. Meanwhile, while they're crossing, you could pretend to lie in wait as the hungry croc, waiting should the player's foot slip on to the trap cushion at any point.
5. Once the player's crossed safely, either they can go again and you choose another word to be the trap cushion, or it's the next player's turn.
6. If at any point they accidentally step on the trap, the crocodile snaps them and pulls them into the water. Our crocodile is VERY tickly!
7. Keep crossing the bridge, changing the trap each time until every cushion has been a trap, and your kids will have done loads of reading without even realizing!

For older ones: Put all the letters for one word inside a balloon – then, when the kids pop each balloon, they have to unscramble the anagram inside!

2

POP!

Some little ones are terrified of balloons popping – this is not the game for them. But some wee daredevils have a penchant for noise and destruction, and love nothing more than making things go bang! This cracker of a game is for them. I invented it to celebrate reaching 20,000 followers on Instagram. Whenever I want to mention something a bit cringe, I like to do it with a game – it distracts everyone, so they don't think, *What a self-congratulatory knob that Five Minute Mum is!*

GRAB:

- a pen and some paper
- some balloons

TO SET UP . . .

1. Write whatever letters you want your child to learn on small bits of paper – it could be the letters of their name, new letters or letters they tend to get stuck on.
2. Fold the bits of paper up small, then push them into the deflated balloons.
3. Blow up the balloons and tie them up.

TO PLAY . . .

1. Explain to your kids that they have to pop the balloons to find the secret inside. How many different ways can they find to pop the balloons?
2. Once they have popped the balloons, ask them to spell out words with the letters. Can they spell their name?

You can also do this with a crayon and a long strip of paper tacked to a wall.

NUMBER JUMP

This game is awesome if you have one of those large blackboards in your house, or a wall painted in blackboard paint. One day I might own my dream house with space for a wall like that, but for now I just have the side of a shed and that's grand with me.

GRAB:

- some chalk
- a bouncy ball (optional)

TO SET UP . . .

1. On a wall, draw a vertical line and write numbers from 1 to 5 (or to 10 or 20, depending on how confident your little one is) in chalk alongside it. Start with 1 at your child's knee height, then move upwards, ending at the highest point you can reach when jumping.
2. Leave the chalk and the bouncy ball (if you're using one) on the ground nearby.

TO PLAY . . .

1. Start by showing children what to do. Holding the chalk in one hand, jump up and draw on the wall as high as you can reach. Where on the number line did you get to? Say the number and put a tick next to it.
2. Now it's your little one's turn. They say the number they reached and tick it off.
3. Once your little one has reached all the numbers they can, give them the bouncy ball. Get them to see if they can bounce it up to a higher number. Alternatively you can lift them up to a different number each time.
4. Keep going until all the numbers have been ticked off.

If you don't have a muffin tray handy, you can use a baking tray or any other kind of tray and place the letters on that.

3+

LETTER QUARRY

Another train game! Is it obvious yet that Ewan just wasn't into letters and absolutely freaking loved trains? No? Oh, goody! Here's another fun steam-engine game, then. As you know, I never force (or even ask) my little ones to 'learn' their letters, but when the time came and Ewan went to school he already knew most of the alphabet. Why 'teach' when you can play for five minutes instead?

GRAB:

- a toy train track and a train with a carriage – if you don't have these, use a toy digger or truck
- magnetic letters – if you don't have any, make some cardboard letters
- a muffin tray
- scissors
- a pen and some paper

TO SET UP . . .

1. Set up a small train track and put the train and carriage on it. The carriage needs to be big enough to hold the letters.
2. At one end of the track, put all the magnetic letters in a pile. This is your 'quarry'.
3. Put the muffin tray at the other end of the track. This end of the track is your 'loading dock', and the tray is your 'shipping container'.
4. Cut out twelve bits of paper small enough to fit into the muffin tray. Write a letter on each piece of paper, and put one in each hole of the muffin tray.

TO PLAY . . .

1. Explain to your little one that the train has an important job to do: it must collect all the letters from the quarry and take them to the loading dock.
2. Play with your little one, loading as many letters as you can at a time on to the carriage.
3. Once the letters are transported back to the loading dock, ask your child whether there are any matches in the muffin-tray shipping container. Get them to pop the letters that match into the correct holes in the shipping container.
4. Keep going until all the letters have been transported to the loading dock.

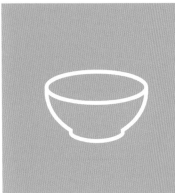

3+

1²₃

MATCHING GAMES

Sometimes the simplest of games are really quite obvious, but we just never think to do them. When you're in the trenches of parenthood, battling through potty-training and cooking healthy meals that you then have to scoop off your floor, it's difficult to function when you're constantly muttering 'Help!' or shouting 'Where are your **SHOES?**' Even the most creative brain crumbles into dust. Sometimes we just need someone to point out the obvious and say, 'Well, what about this?'

NAME MATCH

GRAB:

- a pen and some paper
- scissors
- a bowl

TO SET UP . . .

1. Write your name twice on a bit of paper.
2. Write your child's name twice on a bit of paper.
3. Cut one of each name into individual letters.
4. Fold the letters up and pop them in the bowl.
5. Leave the complete names nearby.

TO PLAY . . .

1. Take it in turns to pull a letter from the bowl.
2. Match it to the letters of the complete names.
3. Keep going until both names are spelled out.

NUMBER PAIRS

GRAB:

- A4 paper or thin card
- scissors
- pen

TO SET UP . . .

1. Fold a piece of A4 paper or card three times to give you eight equal rectangles as shown in the photo on the opposite page.

2. Cut out the rectangles.

3. Write pairs of numbers on the rectangles. So, write 1 on two of the rectangles, then write 2 on two of them, and so on, up to 4.

4. Mix the rectangles up and turn them over, face down, so you can't see the numbers.

TO PLAY . . .

1. Take turns to turn over two rectangles. If you get two that match, you get to keep them.

2. Play until all the rectangles are gone. If one player gets more rectangles than the other they win, or perhaps you'll get two each and it'll be a draw!

3+

abc

LETTER OF THE DAY

For those of you who follow me on social media, this will be very familiar! Every summer, when there is a month left before school begins again, I play Letter of the Day with my kiddies.

I originally started this the year Ewan was beginning school as a way to gently get a bit of daily learning into our routine that would prepare him for his new environment and way of life. Each morning, we chose a letter of the alphabet from a bag, and played a little five-minute game with it. We also had a go at writing it down. I included a wee treat after we had played with our letter each day, sort of like a back-to-school advent calendar.

Ewan really loved it. When the day came to wave him off at the classroom door, I really felt like I'd given him the best possible chance at nailing his first year. Here's how you can do it too.

GRAB:

- all the letters of the alphabet in any form – wooden, foam, magnetic or written on bits of paper
- a box or bag to put the letters in
- a pen and some paper
- a little bag of treats (optional)

TO SET UP . . .

1. Pop all the letters in the box or bag.
2. Leave them somewhere that you can use them every day.

TO PLAY . . .

1. Each morning, let your child choose a letter from the box or bag. Tell them the name of the letter and the sound it makes. (For more about letters and sounds, see page 172.) Have fun saying it in silly ways together. What voices can they do?
2. Now have a go at writing the letter. You write it first, then let your child copy. Do the upper-case and lower-case forms of the letter.
3. Next, try to find something in the house that starts with the letter or has that letter sound in it. For example, for H you might find a hat, but a 'box' for X is also good as long as you emphasize how the sound is at the end of the word.
4. Now let your little one draw a picture of what they found.
5. After this we sometimes also do a little activity with our letter. If you want to, you can give your child one of the treats after you've finished.

Some of my online friends came up with a few of these brilliant ideas! Search #letterofthedaytakeover for more.

HERE ARE 26 IDEAS TO TRY!

1. Make a giant letter with all the shoes in your house.
2. Draw the letter with a stick in some sand or mud in the garden.
3. Find the letter in a Scrabble set. See how many tiles of that letter there are.
4. Draw the letter in chalk on the kitchen floor or outside.
5. Make the letter with stones.
6. Go for a walk together and see how many number plates you can spot the letter on.
7. Write the letter in shaving foam on the bathroom tiles.
8. Write the letter on paper with a white wax crayon, then paint over it with watery paint. What happens?
9. Draw the letter with your finger in a tray of flour.
10. Write the letter on cardboard with a paintbrush dipped in water.
11. Make the letter using toy cars, trains, dolls or small teddies.
12. You write the letter on a window with a whiteboard marker, then get kids to rub it out.
13. Stamp the letter out with your feet in sand on the beach.
14. Find the letter as many times as you can in your child's favourite book.
15. Ask your child to make the letter with their own body. Take photos on your phone to show them what they look like!
16. Go for a walk together and see how many street signs you can spot your chosen letter on.
17. Make the letter with sticks.
18. Write the letter while upside down by sticking a piece of paper to the underside of a table.
19. Get a newspaper or a magazine and a highlighter, and get your child to highlight the letter when they find it on a page.
20. Get your child to write the letter as small as they can and as big as they can.
21. Make the letter using toy food on a picnic blanket.
22. Have a go at cutting the letter out of some paper together.
23. Make a masking-tape track in the shape of the letter.
24. You draw several bubble letters on a page, then get your child to colour in the one that is their letter.
25. Make the letter with your child's favourite cereal or raisins as a snack.
26. Cover a piece of paper with all the letters of the alphabet and use a bingo dotter or highlighter to find your chosen letter.

FIVE TIPS FOR INDEPENDENT PLAY

Independent play is when your child goes off and finds ways to play, discover and explore by themselves, without your support, comment and input. Firstly, let me say this: independent play is JUST as important for your kids as playing with you. They need this solo time throughout the day as much as they need to play, chat or read with you. It's all about finding a balance.

Boredom encourages little brains to create. Your kids need some space and freedom to truly discover themselves. If someone is always there directing them, how will they ever realize what they can do alone? Doing things on their own allows them to build confidence in themselves and in their choices.

SO, HOW DO YOU ENCOURAGE INDEPENDENT PLAY? HERE ARE FIVE IDEAS:

1. PLAY A FIVE-MINUTE GAME FIRST

Before doing anything else, play a quick five-minute game with your child. Give them your full, undivided attention. Doing this first means you can rest assured they've had some time with you when you leave them alone later. They haven't been ignored, and this can keep any parental guilt at bay. Plus, once you've shown them how to play a game, they're much more likely to continue playing it on their own.

2. 'I AM BUSY. GO AND PLAY.'

After my kids and I have played a five-minute game together, I explain that I have jobs to do, then I walk away. If they keep coming up to me, I tell them, 'Mummy is busy. Go and play.' I say this ON REPEAT, while busying myself with whatever jobs need to be done. Eventually, the kids go and play. I love watching them invent better games than I could EVER think up. You might feel bad while you're telling them to go and play, but as soon as you see what they come up with you'll realize it was worth it. They just needed your encouragement. Hold tight!

3. SET IT UP

I often lay out three toys or activities to encourage my kids to play. Nothing big! All I do is find a (slightly less) messy space in the house, then dig out a few toys – for example, a couple of dolls and a blanket, some Duplo blocks and the animal box. It takes five minutes, and you're creating what's often called 'an invitation to play'. Your kids are much more likely to explore the toys themselves if they can see them. Pointing at a shut toy cupboard will only result in cries of 'But I'm bored!' Kids are lazy. Make it simple for them. Make it simple for yourself.

4. USE A TIMER

Timers are great for helping littlies to understand the concept of time. Start small. Put out a couple of toys, then show them the timer and explain how it works. Say, 'I'm busy while this timer is on.' Then set the timer for five minutes and put it somewhere they can see it. Over the weeks, as they get the hang of the idea, you can gradually increase the amount of time. Here's my general rule of thumb: at age two, they can do ten minutes of independent play at a time; at age three, they can do twenty minutes; at age four, they can go for half an hour. (I think I got that off a TV show about kids years ago!)

5. CURB THE INTERRUPTIONS

Often, because we are wonderful, diligent parents, when we see our child playing we comment on what they are doing. 'Look at that tower!' 'What colour is that car you've got?' 'Aren't you doing a great job with those bricks?' We can't help ourselves! It's a natural response – of course it is – and talking is crucial to a child's development. However, when it comes to encouraging independent play, sometimes try not to say anything when you see your child is fully immersed in whatever they're doing. Just watch from a distance, and let them crack on. You don't have to do this every time, but every so often when they are totally engrossed just let them stay in that bubble.

3

'YOU VERSUS ME'

NOTHING LIKE A BIT OF HEALTHY COMPETITION

GIANT SNAKES AND LADDERS
LETTER DICE
OBSTACLE COURSE
BLOW FOOTBALL
SPORTS DAY
LETTER REACTION WALL
WORLD CUP GAME
LIVING-ROOM VOLLEYBALL AND TENNIS
TODDLER PONG
ALPHABET KNOCKDOWN
BALLS AND A BUCKET
HIP-SHAKE TWERK RACE
STEPPING STONES
NEWSPAPER NETBALL
LOUNGE LONG JUMP

NOTHING LIKE A BIT OF HEALTHY COMPETITION

The 'you' I'm referring to in the title of this chapter, dear reader, is your little one – or little ones, if you have two, three, four or even more. (I take my hat off to all of you who carried on after two!) And the 'me' is you, the reader.

Kids are good at bringing a competitive spirit to family games. When it comes to winning and losing in our house, I use a rough 2:1 ratio – for every three games we play, my kids win two and I win one. I don't want to batter their confidence by annihilating them every time, shouting 'Ten–nil to me again, kids!' as I do a shirtless victory dance across the lawn. Nobody – and I mean nobody – wants to see that. But I do want my kids to see me really try. I want them to see me put in effort. I want them to see how I act when I win, so that I can model the sort of behaviour I'd like to see from them when they win, whether it's against me or their friends. After a game, we say things like 'Well played' or **'GIVE ME FIVE'**, regardless of victory or defeat.

Taking turns is a constant theme throughout this chapter. Children are selfish little things, and always want it to be their turn and their way. But the world doesn't work like that, so it's up to us to gently show them how sharing works. Rather than shouting 'Sharing is caring!' at my two little nose-miners as they fight over the same toy again, I instead play turn-taking games with them that demonstrate how it's done. We also have sand timers for sharing toys, because, man, that argument gets old fast!

Some little ones struggle to maintain interest or enthusiasm once they realize they are 'losing' a game. Perseverance is probably the most difficult element of competition to teach, and one of the most helpful words here is **'YET'**. When your kids say, 'I can't do it,' try replying, 'You can't do it YET.' Encourage them by explaining that everyone who is brilliant at something now had to give it a first try once and maybe even got it wrong. We are all beginners at some point, and we only ever win by continuing to try. Make sure you also regularly talk to your kids about the things that you find tricky or get wrong.

The emotions we feel when we're winning, losing, persevering, taking our turn, being patient, experiencing disappointment or feeling like a champion are essential parts of life. If we show our little ones how to handle these emotions through play, then we set them up in the best way possible for the realities of the big wide world. And what better way to do that than with a few bits and bobs you've grabbed from around the house, the **GOLDEN RULE** and the magic words 'Do you want to play?'

For these games, if you don't have space at home, you could try some of them in the local park!

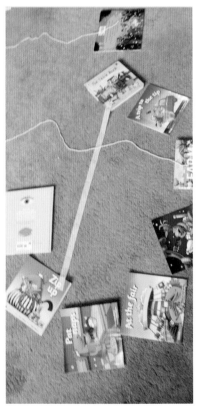

For little ones learning to read: Add some additional squares with bits of paper that say things like 'hop 5 times' or 'go back 3 steps' – whatever you like!

3+

123

GIANT SNAKES AND LADDERS

I love dice. There are so many games you can play with them, and counting the dots from one to six is such a great early skill. I always have several dice kicking around the house so I can grab one if I'm stuck for ideas. This game came to me miraculously, right when the kids were driving me freaking bonkers and I was fed up with muttering 'FFS' to myself.

GRAB:

- a load of books or cushions (about 25)
- a length of string (or more if you want more 'snakes')
- masking tape
- a dice

TO SET UP . . .

1. Scatter the books or cushions across a room in a rough, wiggly line – these are your 'board-game squares'.
2. Between two of your squares, lay down a wiggly line of string – this is your 'snake'. You can have one or a few 'snakes'.
3. Between another two squares, stick down some masking tape – this is your 'ladder'. (It doesn't have to actually look like a ladder! It can be just a line. But you can make rungs too, if you're feeling fancy.) Again, you can have one or more ladders.

TO PLAY . . .

1. Err . . . pretty self-explanatory, yes?! Just take it in turns to throw the dice and jump across the corresponding number of board squares. (You are the 'counters'!)
2. If you land on a snake, you go back to the square at the end of the snake.
3. If you land on a ladder, you go forward to the square at the top of the ladder.
4. The first player to reach the finishing line wins!

Add a dice per player to include more letters.

See how many words you can make out of the letters at the end of the game!

LETTER DICE

For a wee while, it seemed as though everyone I knew had those foam alphabet mats on their floor. You know, the kind that slot together and are all bright colours. I saw some for sale secondhand and because, you know, FOMO, I bought them but I didn't have anywhere to put them. So I started thinking up games I could use them in. Once I'd figured out how to make them into a cube . . . well, the game wrote itself.

GRAB:

- 6 foam letter tiles that connect together (if you don't have any, write random letters on cardboard to make some)
- masking tape (if using cardboard tiles)
- a pen and some paper

TO SET UP . . .

1. Turn the foam letter tiles into dice by connecting them into a cube. If you are using cardboard letter tiles, tape them together into a cube.
2. Write your name on one bit of paper, and write your little one's name on another.
3. Write each letter of the dice on a piece of paper, so you can circle each one when a player gets it. Depending on how able your kids are, you could also leave the page blank and let them write the letters themselves when they roll them.

TO PLAY . . .

1. Take it in turns to throw the dice.
2. Each player circles the letter they have rolled on their piece of paper (or they can write it down).
3. The winner is the first player to get all the letters!

Change the order of the obstacles. Ask your kids whether they think this will make them quicker or slower, then see if they are right. A bit of science fun!

Get your kids to time you! This is a great way to get number recognition and writing into a game for more physical learners.

OBSTACLE COURSE

The brilliance of this game is that your kids can compete against themselves while you actually sit down for a few minutes! The first time we set up an obstacle course for my two we were at my parents' house. We'd had a full-on day and were all shattered, gasping for a cuppa and a rest, but Ewan was having none of it. So we plonked some cushions and a footstool around the living room, then took it in turns to 'time' him. While he burned off all that excess energy, the rest of us enjoyed a brew.

GRAB:

- around 10 things to use as obstacles – cushions as stepping stones, books as hurdles, an empty box as a tunnel, footstools to clamber over, washing baskets to throw balls into, teddies to weave around . . . Anything you like!
- a scoreboard – you can use pens and paper, a blackboard, a whiteboard or a Magna Doodle
- a stopwatch or timer

TO SET UP . . .

1. Lay your obstacles out across a room or your garden.
2. Put the scoreboard and timer nearby.

TO PLAY . . .

1. Demonstrate how to complete the obstacle course by weaving in and out of or going over and under things.
2. Explain to your kids that you're going to time them and write down their scores. The idea is to complete the obstacle course as quickly as possible.
3. Say, 'On your marks, get set, go!' then start the timer.
4. When they're finished, show them their score. Write it on the scoreboard together.
5. Repeat as many times as you like, taking turns. Can they get faster? Can they beat you?

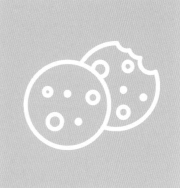

Ewan was always reluctant to write, so keeping score was a great way to get him to put pen to paper without realizing it!

BLOW FOOTBALL

When I first started my blog, my cousin's wife asked me to think up some games for her son, Henry, who is Ewan's age and has cystic fibrosis (a hereditary condition that affects his lungs). He has to do daily exercises that involve blowing and emptying his lungs, and his mum thought games would make this chore a bit more fun. So I came up with three blowing games and published them in a post called 'Henry's Games', which I've continued to add to over the years. Just like his dad, Henry loves football, so this is one of the first games I suggested. It's fun for everyone at the same time as helping out the little legend who is Henry. (You can find more of these blowing games on page 203.)

GRAB:

- masking tape
- 2 plastic or paper cups
- 2 straws
- a small ball or a scrunched-up bit of paper or foil
- a scoreboard – you can use pens and paper, a blackboard, a whiteboard or a Magna Doodle

TO SET UP . . .
1. Tape the cups to opposite ends of a low kid-height table.
2. Put the straws, ball and scoreboard nearby.

TO PLAY . . .
1. Pop the ball in the middle of the table. One player goes at each end of the table, and takes a straw each.
2. Say 'Go!' Then both players blow through their straws to move the ball across the table. The aim is to score goals by getting the ball into the other player's cup.
3. When someone scores a goal, write it next to their name on the scoreboard. The winner is the person who scores the most goals.

To build excitement, I often try to make the competition a draw until the final race – which the kids usually 'win'!

What races did you do at sports day? Add in spacehoppers or hoops – whatever you like!

SPORTS DAY

Now, these activities will either seem like lots of fun or your idea of hell! I am very aware that, for some, school sports day was the worst day of the year, whereas others (like me) wished it happened every week. Here, I use elements of a traditional sports day to keep my little ones entertained in the garden and also so that I can relive some of my best childhood memories. Forget the kids – I'm winning this beanbag race!

GRAB:

- chalk
- a spoon for each player
- a small ball or bit of scrunched-up foil for each player
- a large hard-wearing bag for each player (for example, reusable shopping bags)
- a small beanbag for each player – if you don't have any, use sandwich bags containing a handful of rice
- a length of string or ribbon for each player
- a scoreboard (optional) – you can use pens and paper, a blackboard, a whiteboard or a Magna Doodle

TO SET UP . . .

1. Make a starting line and a finishing line using chalk, or by placing items as markers.
2. Lay out the equipment for each 'event'. Put the spoons with the small balls or scrunched-up foil. Put the large bags in a pile. Line up the beanbags on the ground. Lay out the string.

TO PLAY . . .

1. For the egg-and-spoon race, players balance their ball or bit of foil on a spoon and race to the finishing line.
2. For the sack race, each player stands inside a large bag and jumps to the finishing line.
3. For the beanbag race, players balance a beanbag on their head and race to the finishing line without dropping it.
4. For the three-legged race, show your kids how to join your ankle and theirs by tying string around them. No winner for this one – it's just for giggles!
5. And don't forget the sprint finish: one final race where you just run!

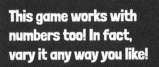
For little ones: Make the letters different colours, and just shout out the colours for them to bash.

This game works with numbers too! In fact, vary it any way you like!

LETTER REACTION WALL

For Ewan's fourth birthday we went to LEGOLAND Discovery Centre. They had a reaction wall there – the type that lights up and you have to bash the light as fast as you can with your hands. We all had a go, and I added another line to the 'game ideas' notes on my phone. This game has been a favourite ever since, and even resulted in me travelling to London with a spatula in my handbag to demonstrate it on live TV. Quite a strange activity for a Thursday afternoon, but, hey, any excuse for a coffee in peace!

GRAB:

- plastic or magnetic letters – if you don't have any, write some on paper and cut them out (around 6 will do)
- Blu-Tack
- something to whack with – a plastic kitchen spatula or a fly swat is ideal
- a scoreboard – you can use pens and paper, a blackboard, a whiteboard or a Magna Doodle
- a stopwatch or timer

TO SET UP . . .

1. Stick six or so letters to a door or wall with the Blu-Tack.
2. Put all the other items nearby.

TO PLAY . . .

1. Explain to your child that you're going to set the timer going and shout out letters. They have to hit the correct letter as fast as they can. (Take turns if more than one child is playing.)
2. Set the timer for thirty seconds or one minute and say 'Go!'
3. Each time your child hits the correct letter, put a tick or a tally line next to their name on the scoreboard.
4. When their time is up, call out 'Stop!' and count their score.
5. Now it's your turn! Show your little one how to start the timer, then get them to shout out letters and add your points to the scoreboard.
6. Let your kids have a second go. Can they beat you? Can they beat themselves?

This is another game that you can play with numbers or letters.

Don't forget to have a presentation ceremony and kiss the trophy!

WORLD CUP GAME

It's coming home! Got a footie-mad little one? This game is for them. My dad and husband both love their football, so anything that encourages the kids to join them for a kick-about in the garden is to be highly recommended. (It also means I am left alone for five minutes!) I invented this game as a sort of Father's Day present one year – it saved me doing paint handprints again, anyway!

GRAB:

- 10 foam letter tiles – if you don't have any, write some letters on bits of cardboard
- a goal (I use a washing basket turned on its side)
- a football
- an old trophy or a cup covered in foil

TO SET UP . . .

1. Plonk the letters around the garden at random.
2. Place the 'goal' at one end of the garden and the ball at the opposite end.
3. Put the trophy in a prominent position.

TO PLAY . . .

1. Tell the kids that you're all in a team, and the trophy is the World Cup!
2. Launch the ball into the air (or roll it into the playing space), then shout out a letter. Your child has to find that letter, dribble the ball round it using small, controlled kicks, then score by kicking the ball into the 'goal'.
3. Next, it's your turn! Your child throws the ball and shouts out a letter, and you do the same.
4. Once every letter has been covered, you've scored ten goals – and your team has won the World Cup!

Players can hit the balloon as many times as they like to get it over the net, so long as it doesn't touch the floor on their side.

LIVING-ROOM VOLLEYBALL AND TENNIS

For lots of little ones, it takes a long time to learn how to catch a ball, and playing 'catch' frustrates them really quickly. However, a nice big balloon moves much slower than a ball! Use a balloon to play a bit of volleyball or tennis in your front room or in the garden (if it isn't too windy – no one needs tears as the balloon flies away!) and let your kids really get the hang of catching or hitting a moving object.

GRAB:

- a load of cushions (enough to lay together to divide your playing space in half)
- a balloon (and maybe some spare balloons in case it pops!)
- a paper or plastic plate for each player
- a scoreboard – you can use pens and paper, a blackboard, a whiteboard or a Magna Doodle

TO SET UP . . .

1. Create a 'net' by dividing the room or garden in half with cushions.
2. Put the balloon, plates and scoreboard nearby.

TO PLAY . . .

1. Explain to your kids that one player goes on either side of the 'net'. The idea is to hit the balloon over the net and get it to touch the floor on the other side.
2. For volleyball, hit the balloon with your hands. For tennis, use a plate as a racket to hit the balloon.
3. A player gets a point every time the balloon touches the ground on their opponent's side. Mark the points on the scoreboard.
4. The first player to get five points wins!

To practise colour recognition: Use different-coloured cups or put different-coloured items inside each cup. This is good for ages one to three.

To practise letter or number recognition: Write letters or numbers on the cups with a whiteboard pen or a pencil. You could also pop a letter or number from a set inside. Great for ages three to four.

To practise writing: Pop a letter or number inside each cup. Grab a piece of paper and draw a box for each of the letters or numbers. Each time a player gets one, they have to write it in the box. The first player to fill all their boxes wins!

Get competitive with a set of cups at opposite ends of a table!

TODDLER PONG

This game came from my hen do. My lovely girls know me well, so the weekend was full of brilliant games, including 'Prosecco pong' which ended with my mum cheating and everyone crying with laughter. When I arrived home in a bedraggled state, I discovered a ping-pong ball in my handbag. *Hey*, I thought, *the kids might like a go at this*. (Minus the Prosecco, of course – but I was off it for quite a while, anyway!)

GRAB:

- some paper or plastic cups
- a pen and some paper
- scissors
- a ping-pong ball or bouncy ball

TO SET UP . . .

1. Pop the cups on the floor. They can be dotted about randomly, in a line or in a triangle.
2. Write something you'd like your little one to practise on a piece of paper, then cut it out and put it in a cup. For example, if they're learning particular letters or numbers, write them down. Do this for all the cups.
3. Put the ball nearby.

TO PLAY . . .

1. Explain to your little one that the idea is to bounce the ball and try to get it to land in one of the cups. (Take turns if you're playing with more than one child.)
2. When a player gets the ball into a cup, they can take out the bit of paper and see what it is. Help them to read it out loud, then remove that cup.
3. Keep playing until all the cups are gone.

Always use a combination of letters that your child is familiar with (such as the letters in their name) and some new letters.

This obviously works just as well with numbers!

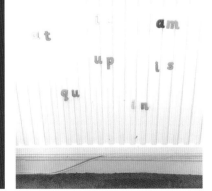

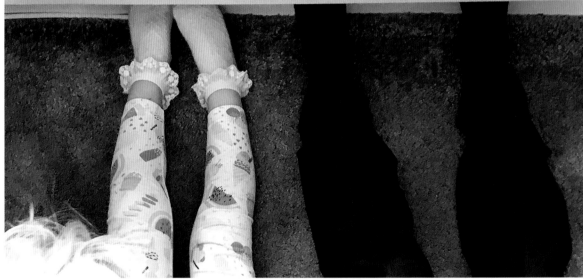

ALPHABET KNOCKDOWN

Magnetic letters and numbers are a crucial part of my toolkit (see page 7). Like blocks, they are so handy to have because you can play with them in so many different ways. In our house, playing usually involves some form of competition or destruction. If I can wedge letter or colour learning into it, as we lob balls across the room, then all the better! The idea is for the kids to have so much fun they don't even realize they're learning.

GRAB:

- magnetic letters (about three or four per player) – if you don't have any, make some cardboard letters and stick them to the wall with Blu-Tack
- a small ball (a squash ball is ideal)

TO SET UP . . .

1. Stick the letters to a radiator or the fridge. If you're using cardboard letters, tack them loosely to a door or wall.
2. Leave the ball nearby and await your children's interest!

TO PLAY . . .

1. Each player sits at leg's length from where the letters are. This means that littler kids will be closer.
2. Take it in turns to throw the ball at the letters and try to knock one down. Players say which letter they are aiming for. If a player knocks a letter down, they get to keep it.
3. Once all the letters have been knocked down, count them to see who has the most. Don't forget to ask each player to say all their letters – the more kids hear and say those letter names, the better.

You could go on and on inventing ways to play with a bucket and some balls. Can your kids think up another game?

Don't forget to count your balls, shouting out the numbers from one through to five. Might as well do some number learning as you go!

BALLS AND A BUCKET

Now, this will surprise you as much as it did me, but I played these games with three-year-old Florence while mildly hungover after a night away with friends. If I need to lie down, I often play first so I can wallow in front of the TV guilt-free, happily knowing the kids have had some attention. This particular day was a sunny one, though, so off we went into the garden, where there just happened to be a bucket and some balls lying around . . .

GRAB:

- 5 small balls for each player
- a spoon for each player
- a bucket

TO SET UP . . .

1. Pop the balls into piles for each player. Place the spoons in a pile nearby.
2. Put the bucket about ten small paces away from the balls.

TO PLAY . . .

1. For the first game, players run and drop their balls into the bucket one at a time.
2. For the second game, players do the same, but carry each ball in an item of clothing they're wearing.
3. For the third game, players carry each ball in a spoon, like an egg-and-spoon race.
4. For the fourth game, tip the bucket on its side. Players then kick their balls into the bucket one at a time.
5. For the fifth game, players stand three paces away from the bucket and throw their balls into it one at a time.
6. For all these games, the first player to get all five of their balls into the bucket wins.

The littler the player, the larger the hole in their box needs to be for the paper to jump out of – this will make it easier.

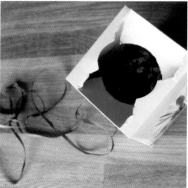

HIP-SHAKE TWERK RACE

At Christmas we do something called 'table presents'. This just means that whoever isn't hosting buys silly, fun presents for each person round the dinner table. Last year, I got someone a game called Twerk Pong. The kids loved it, and we all had a good giggle at them bouncing around the room. It occurred to me that we could turn this into a game – one perfect for wearing out energetic kids so the grown-ups can zonk out in front of the telly afterwards with a tin of choccies.

GRAB:

- a small box (for example, an empty tissue box) for each player (basically you need a box that has a big hole in the top, or that's open at the top)
- a length of string or ribbon for each player
- 5 bits of scrunched-up paper for each player

TO SET UP . . .

1. Poke two holes near the top of the boxes, then thread the string through them. The string needs to be long enough to tie up round each player's waist.
2. Pop five bits of screwed-up paper inside each box.

TO PLAY . . .

1. Tie a box round each player's waist.
2. Say, 'Ready, steady, go!'
3. Each player jumps and twists and shakes, trying to make the bits of paper jump out of their box.
4. The winner is the first player to lose all their bits of paper.

For very little ones: Just jumping along the cushions with you, shouting 'One, two, three . . .' as they go, is perfect!

STEPPING STONES

DON'T STEP ON THE LAVA!!! Did you play this as a kid? Did you turn cushions into stepping stones, then try to cross the living room without touching the carpet, which was imaginary molten rock? This is a great game to try if you've got kids of different ages, as there are so many fantastic ways to vary it depending on ability.

GRAB:

- 6 cushions
- 6 items to learn per player – it could be colours, letters, numbers, words or digraphs (see page 173 for more about digraphs)
- a dice

TO SET UP . . .

1. Plonk the cushions out in a line – these are your 'stepping stones'.
2. Pop one item you want your kids to learn alongside each cushion. There should be one item to learn per player beside each cushion.
3. Put the dice nearby.

TO PLAY . . .

1. When your kids spot the fun-looking game you've laid out for them, explain how it works. Players take turns to roll the dice, then jump across the corresponding number of stepping stones.
2. They win the item that's alongside the cushion they've landed on. After they've said what it is (for example, *red*, *five* or the letter T), they can pop their prize in their pile.
3. The first player to collect all six of their items wins!
4. Keep playing until everyone has collected all six of their items.

Screwing up newspaper is a fab way for kids to work the hand muscles needed for tricky fine motor skills like holding a pencil.

NEWSPAPER NETBALL

We still get a free weekly newspaper delivered, and all I think when it arrives is, *Hurrah, a free play resource!* It's handy for covering the table for painting (which we only do about once a month) and for making papier mâché (which, in my case, we do once a lifetime!), but mostly it's great for screwing up into a ball and throwing! The best bit about this game is that the clean-up involves simply chucking everything into the recycling bin. Win!

GRAB:

- a pen and some paper
- three buckets, large bowls or washing baskets
- a newspaper

TO SET UP . . .

1. Write the numbers 1, 2 and 3 on three bits of paper.
2. Pop the three buckets out and stand the numbers in front of them.
3. Put out a little pile of six pieces of newspaper per player.

TO PLAY . . .

1. Each player sits by their pile of newspaper.
2. Say, 'Ready, steady, go!'
3. Each player then screws each bit of paper into a ball and throws it into a bucket. One ball goes in the bucket labelled 1, two balls go into bucket 2, and three balls into bucket 3.
4. The first player to get all six of their balls into the buckets correctly wins.

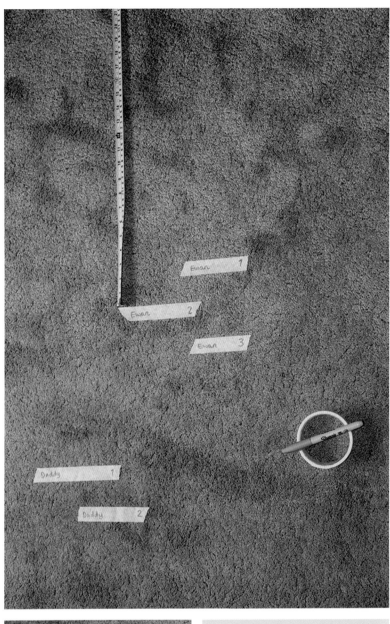

Do a slow clap at the start to build pre-jump excitement!

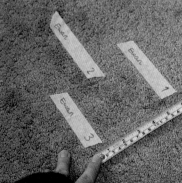

LOUNGE LONG JUMP

I take absolutely no credit at all for this one. Much like the name Five Minute Mum, the brains behind this is my husband, Ewan and Florence's wonderful dad, who often plays fun games too but just doesn't blog about it! After we'd watched some athletics on TV, Ewan wanted to show us how far he could jump, so Daddy set this up for him.

GRAB:

- masking tape
- a measuring tape
- a pen

TO SET UP . . .

1. Plonk all your items down in the room in your home that has the most space.

TO PLAY . . .

1. Put a bit of tape down and explain to your little ones that this is where they start their run-up.
2. Put down another bit of tape to mark the jumping board, and explain that their toes mustn't cross this line.
3. Your kids then take turns to run and jump as far as they can. Pop a bit of masking tape down wherever they land.
4. Use the measuring tape to see how far it was, and write down the distance on the tape that marks their jump.
5. Let them jump again. Can they beat their last jump?

FIVE MINUTE MUM
TRIANGLES

You can't do it all. Oh no you can't. You can't play five-minute games and have a perfect house and cook a nutritious meal from scratch and put a wash on and reply to your emails and have a baby constantly on your hip and phone to make a dentist appointment. Nope. Not possible. You are not an octopus. If you try to do all these things at once, you will collapse in a heap. (Or become dependent on something which, quite frankly, isn't compatible with children. More's the shame, eh?)

One evening, as I stood at the kitchen worktop stuffing last night's biriyani into my gob, I felt the guilt creeping in. We had spent the afternoon doing Ewan's homework, then I had sat and cuddled Flo, who was a bit grumpy after a nap. Doing these things meant that 5 p.m. had swung round (dinner time over here) and I'd turned to the fridge in desperation and microwaved the leftover takeaway for myself and given the kids beans on toast. It was hardly the wholesome family mealtime I had always envisioned as a parent of two . . .

Then I thought, No. Hang on a mother-fudging minute. I've done homework with Ewan, and I've chatted and played with him. I've cuddled my two-year-old until she was happy again. I am doing all right here.

So where was that stupid guilt coming from?

I drew myself a triangle. In one corner, I wrote 'Cuddling Flo'; in another, I put 'Doing homework' (with Ewan); on the third, 'Home-cooked meal'. Then in the middle I wrote 'PICK TWO'. I circled the ones we had done.

You can't do it all. Just pick two.

Now, when I'm in a similar pickle, I draw a mental triangle in my head. I say to myself, 'You can only pick two.' One ball has to get dropped. Which is it to be? On another day, I might have cuddled Flo and cooked something nutritious that we all ate together, but left out Ewan's homework. Or perhaps I would have prioritized the homework and the dinner got done, but Flo had to be grumpy at my feet while I chopped up the veg. The triangle won't ever be the same.

Don't try to triangle whole days. Just do those little moments when you feel you are being pulled in three directions and are starting to feel bad that you aren't doing everything.

I hope these triangles help you. I often pop them up on social media, as a little reminder of how important it is to protect ourselves as the caregivers of small humans. It's a lot.

You can't do it all.

Home-cooked meal

PICK TWO

Doing homework

Cuddling Flo

If you are struggling to cope, please speak to your family doctor, or in the UK ring the Samaritans for free on 116 123.

GETTING
SCHOOL-READY

STARTING SCHOOL

DRESSING GAMES
PENNY NAME
TWO HOOPS
THE CODE-BREAKER
POSTIE FUN
THE LETTER MONSTER
THE SHOP
JUNK-MAIL HUNTING
THE NUMBER THIEF
DOT-TO-DOT WHODUNNIT
LETTER DIGGERS
PIRATE TREASURE MAP
SPIDER'S WEB
CRACK THE EGG
SILLY SOUP
'TELL ME A STORY FROM YOUR HEAD'

STARTING SCHOOL

The cliché is true: one minute you're on high alert to catch milky burps, then you blink and you've got a four-year-old who is trying on a school jumper and regularly tells you that you smell like poo.

All of a sudden there I was, a 'school parent'. I felt almost as daunted and nervous and excited as my little dude did about the new adventure looming ahead. In the summer before Ewan started school, I wrote a blog post about the things we'd done to prepare for the big event – and, in all honesty, it probably didn't include much of what you might expect.

Teachers expect children to start school not knowing anything at all, and will teach letters and counting right from the beginning. Teachers are there to support the children in their classes all the way through, so it's not at all required for a child to be able to write the alphabet perfectly on their first day. Instead, the skills children will find useful in school are way more basic than you might think! Stuff like:

- get dressed by themselves
- go to the toilet by themselves
- ask for help when they need it
- recognize their own name
- cope with anxiety.

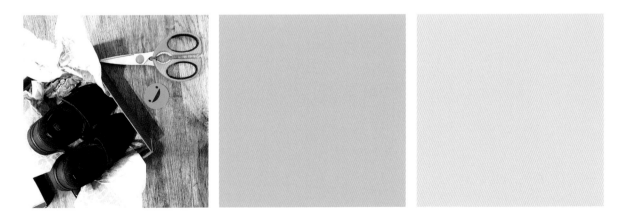

So, here are my tips for helping your little ones with these things!

GETTING DRESSED

The ratio of adults to children in a school is often very different from the ratio at nursery. School teachers don't have time to help every child zip up their coat or put their trousers back on after PE. Ideally your wee one needs to be able to do as much as they can for themselves when it comes to putting on or removing their clothing.

Here are some ideas that I have used with my kids.

- To help your child put their school shoes on the correct feet, cut a sticker in half then pop one half inside each shoe. This will help them to work out which shoe goes on the left and which one goes on the right.
- To practise putting on trickier items of clothing, play the games on pages 137–139 of this chapter.
- Put out dressing-up stuff at home for your child to play with. You could even let them try on some of your clothes for fun!

GOING TO THE TOILET

In the months leading up to your child starting school, I recommend having regular five-minute chats with them about it. Little and often is always best. And during one of those chats explain that in school they might need to ask a grown-up to use the toilet and that those grown-ups aren't there to wipe their little bums, and they'll have to remember to wash their hands on their own. Here's a song I've found quite helpful (sung to the tune of 'Row, Row, Row Your Boat'):

Wash, wash, wash your hands
Scrub them nice and clean
In and out and round and round
Make those handies gleam!

ASKING FOR HELP

This can be quite a difficult skill to teach. If my little ones get frustrated at not being able to do something when we are playing a game together or learning something new, I calmly attempt to explain that there's no need to get cross if you can ask for help.

It goes something like this:

- Your child tries to do something, but they can't do it.
- You say, 'What are you going to do next?'
- They say, 'You do it.'
- You say, 'Why don't you ask me for some help?' Wait for them to ask. You might prompt them with something like, 'Go on. Ask away!'
- They say, 'Can you help me, please?'
- You say, 'Yes, of course!' Give them a big smile, then support them to do it.
- Remind them that, if they ask nicely, people are always willing to help.
- Next time they get stuck, simply say, 'So what do we need to do?' Eventually, they'll reply along the lines of 'ask for help'.

Now, obviously this twee little example isn't exactly how it goes! But you get the idea. I keep this template in my head and use it to guide the conversation. I hope that when the time comes at school they might think, *What can I do next?* and that 'ask for help' is what automatically pops into their little heads.

RECOGNIZING THEIR OWN NAME

Although it's wonderful if your child can write their own name, they don't necessarily need to be able to do so. Simply being able to spot their own name is a really helpful skill. Luckily, I have a load of games throughout this book to encourage just that! You might start with Target Practice (page 63) like I did with Ewan, and then perhaps try Alphabet Car Park (page 53).

COPING WITH ANXIETY

It is totally natural for children to feel anxious or daunted about starting school. Here are a few little things that might help.

- **HEARTS:** Draw a small heart on the palm of your child's hand, then draw a matching one on your own palm. (If you're worried it might wash off, you could also draw it on your wrists.) Explain that, any time your child feels worried, they can press the special love heart on their hand and it will send a magic cuddle to you – and you will send one back! Practise doing this while you're sitting together, pressing your hearts then giving each other a cuddle. Do this a couple of days before your child starts school, then remember to draw a heart on their palm on their first morning.

- **CALM CHATS:** Every few days, take five minutes to have a quiet moment with your child. Switch off the telly and remove any distractions, and just have a little chat about all the lovely things they will do at school. Mention their favourite things, and talk about what you know your child will really enjoy at school. You might want to mention painting, football, the playground, home corner or other friends who are going to the same school. Ask them to tell you what they think they will find at school. Tell them what you enjoyed most when you went to school.

- **BOOKS OR TV SHOWS ABOUT STARTING SCHOOL:** There are loads of really lovely ones out there! Find books at a local shop or the library, and check online for TV shows.

- **PRACTISE THE TRIP TO SCHOOL:** Practise the walk or drive there together before school begins, and explain that this is what you're doing. If you walk, point out the things you see so that they start to feel familiar. Take a little treat for the journey home again, so it feels like a positive experience. If your child is walking along chatting about school and eating chocolate buttons, they'll associate this happy time with school.

- **QUALITY TIME:** A week before Ewan started school, I put Flo in nursery for a day, then spent time with just my big boy, doing whatever he wanted. We went to the cinema and ate pick-and-mix, then went and had pizza for lunch. Some people call focusing on one child like that 'love-bombing', but I call it tearfully eating a margherita while remembering how my son's chubby little fists used to grab rice cakes and wondering, **WHERE DID THE TIME GO?**

Here in England, the first year of school gets called 'reception' for a reason. It's a 'welcome' year. It's a 'let's get settled into this new way of life' year. Everyone needs to find their feet, including us grown-ups. So go easy on yourself and on your little ones. Spend those first few weeks just chilling out after school. And turn up at the gates with a snack! Remember, this is really just the beginning of the next big adventure.

DRESSING GAMES

Florence loves nothing more than to get herself dressed. From the age of two, she would push me away crossly and say, 'Me, me, me!' if I even dared try to put her leggings on. Ewan, on the other hand, once pretended his own legs didn't work when I asked him to put his underpants on himself. (I had to do that thing where you turn away because you're trying to be serious with them, but dying to laugh.) Ewan needed quite the bucketload of encouragement. And what's the best way to encourage a child? Play!

COAT RACE

This is a great trick for helping little ones put on their coats. It spares the whole 'dog chasing its own tail' effect that usually happens when they try to get that second arm in.

GRAB:

- your child's coat
- your coat

TO SET UP . . .

1. Lay the coats out on the floor.

TO PLAY . . .

1. Get your child to stand in front of their coat so that the hood or collar is at their feet. Explain that they have to lean forward and put their arms into the arm holes, then stand up and lift the coat over their head. Put on your coat, following that method, to show them what to do. There are plenty of videos that demonstrate how to do this on YouTube (search for 'putting coat on').
2. Once they've mastered this method, line up as many coats as you can find on the floor. Who can put all the coats on? Who can do it the quickest? On your marks, get set, race!

If your little ones struggle with putting socks on their feet, let them start with socks on their hands to get used to it.

You can also play this with your names written in chalk, instead of lines!

SOCK CHALK GAME

Not sure about you, but the day I do a load of laundry that doesn't have at least one odd sock will be cause for GREAT celebration. Here's a game to put those perpetual odd socks to use.

GRAB:

- chalk
- a pair of old socks for each player

TO SET UP . . .

1. Find a hard floor that you can chalk on to (do a little test first to be sure).
2. Use the chalk to draw two long lines on the floor.
3. Leave the socks nearby.

TO PLAY . . .

1. Everyone starts with bare feet.
2. Explain that players must put on their socks as fast as they can, then rub out their chalk line. The first player to rub out their line wins!

DRESS THE CHAIR

As a kid, I once saw an episode of *Mr. Bean* in which he put clothes on a chair. I found it so hilarious I used to do it every time I got changed for PE at school. I'd carefully put my school shirt on the back of the chair and pull my skirt over the front legs, so that it looked like the chair was wearing my clothes. Eventually the whole class did it. The teacher must have loved me! Well, why not get your little one to do it for a giggle?

Grab a chair, then let them get undressed and put their clothes on a chair. Then get them to put their clothes back on again.

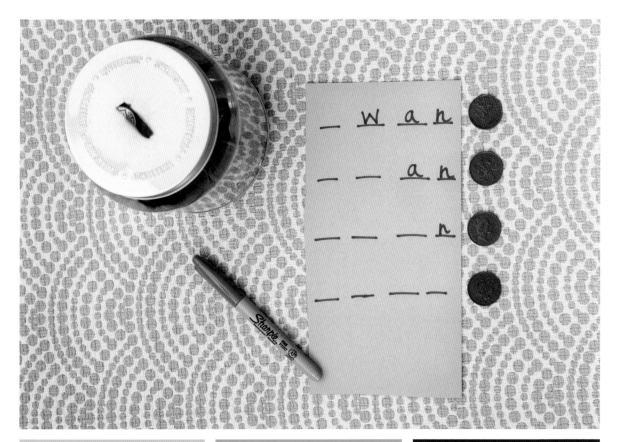

For older ones: This is a great way to practise spelling! If your child is very confident, fold the paper each time they complete a row, so that they have to remember the missing letters instead of copying them.

For a special treat, make the last penny a chocolate coin!

PENNY NAME

The first time I tried this game with Ewan, it was not a hit. He got frustrated and bored quickly. As I've already said, if you aren't all aboard the fun bus, then get the hell off! Even so, I like to give games another go if they might not have worked at first, perhaps when the kids are in a different mood or a few months older. We all feel a bit meh occasionally, while on other days we're driving that fun bus in full clown get-up!

GRAB:

- a pen and some paper
- a handful of pennies (enough for each letter in your child's name)
- a piggy bank (if you don't have one, any box with a slot for money will work)

TO SET UP . . .

1. Write your child's name across the top of the piece of paper. Depending on their confidence, you can write either their first name or their full name. Draw a line beneath each letter.
2. On a line below, write your child's name again, but leave out one letter. Again, draw lines beneath each letter, including one for the missing letter.
3. Repeat this, removing one additional letter each time, until you have a final row at the bottom of the page with only blank letter spaces.
4. Pop a penny at the end of each row. (You should have the same number of rows as there are letters in your child's name.)

TO PLAY . . .

1. Explain to your children that they need to write their name on each row. They start at the top, with the row where only one letter is missing.
2. Each time they complete a row, they get to pop the penny at the end of that row in the piggy bank.
3. Keep going until all the pennies are in the piggy bank, and they have written their name in full.

There are loads of fun ways to match items and letters. Try doing it as a treasure hunt too!

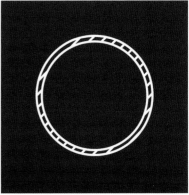

4+

abc

TWO HOOPS

In phonics, the first part of learning letters is being able to identify sounds. (If you're thinking *WTF?* skip to page 172.) However, before children learn the sounds of letters, they can practise listening for *any* kind of sound – a lawnmower, a bicycle bell, animal noises or the sweet sound of their bedroom door closing at 7 p.m. If children are used to listening for more general sounds, it will help them to hear the sounds that letters make. And it's all well and good to know what sound letters make, but can they hear those sounds in a word? Let's play a game and find out!

GRAB:

- 2 large hula hoops or a small container or bowl (if you aren't using hoops)
- 5 small toys or items
- 5 plastic or magnetic letters that match the toys or items – if you don't have any, write some on paper and cut them out

TO SET UP . . .

1. Put the hoops on the ground and cross them over in the middle so there is an empty oval space between them. If you don't have hoops, put a container on the ground.
2. Put the toys or items in one hoop, or to one side of the container.
3. Put the letters in the other hoop, or to the other side of the container.

TO PLAY . . .

1. Ask children to choose a toy or a letter. Ask them to say the name of the letter or toy out loud, then match it with its corresponding letter or toy. For example, if they pick a toy train, they should match it with the letter T, or vice versa.
2. If they get it right, they put both the toy and the letter in the oval between the hoops or in the container.
3. If they struggle, go through each item with them. For example, for a train, say, 'Can you hear a "t" in this word?', then emphasize the letter sound. Let them answer 'yes' or 'no'.
4. Once they've got all five, play again using different items and letters.

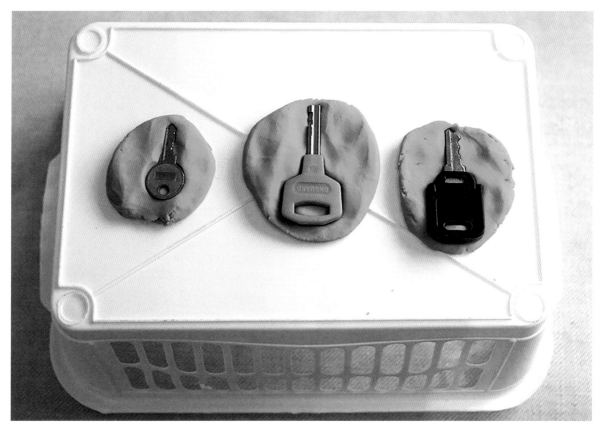

If you don't have a dice, make a spinner with a bit of cardboard and a pencil through it (see page 59) or draw dice–style dots on pieces of paper and draw them out of a hat.

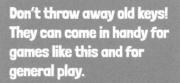

Don't throw away old keys! They can come in handy for games like this and for general play.

THE CODE—BREAKER

This is probably the most popular game from my blog, because it's got a pretty cool name and seems to set the kids' imaginations running wild – the way playtime always should. Plus, it gets them to practise writing numbers without ever realizing that's what they're doing. You'll need to grab quite a few bits and bobs for this one, but hopefully, as always, it's all stuff you already have at home.

GRAB:

- a small toy your child likes – we use Dennis the Dinosaur!
- a little basket or box
- play dough or Blu-Tack
- 3 differently shaped keys
- a pencil and some paper
- a dice

TO SET UP . . .

1. Put the toy under the upside-down basket or box.
2. Make three balls out of the play dough or Blu-Tack, then press a key into each one to make an impression. Put the three key impressions on top of the basket or box.
3. At the top of one bit of paper, trace round one of the keys with the pencil. Draw three boxes below it. Then repeat for the remaining two keys.
4. Leave the dice near the basket or box.
5. Finally hide the keys around the room.

TO PLAY . . .

1. Tell your child that their toy has been trapped inside a cage. They need to set the toy free! In order to do this, they need to find the keys to the cage – and the keys are hidden somewhere in the room!
2. When they find a key, they must match the key to its outline on one of the bits of paper. Let them find the correct bit of paper by matching the key shape.
3. Before they can use the key to unlock the cage, they must roll three numbers on the dice to get the code. They then write the code on the piece of paper. Let them roll the dice, recognize the number and write it in a box.
4. Once they have written down the complete code, they can put the key in its play-dough impression.
5. Repeat with the remaining two keys.
6. When they complete the third key, the cage is unlocked and the toy is released! They will also have written out nine numbers, and hopefully laughed their little socks off.

POSTIE FUN

Postman Pat has really stood the test of time, hasn't he? Amazing, really, considering how incompetent he is when it comes to his occupation! But, seriously, the reason he's still so loved by kids today is because pushing letters and parcels into a box and watching them disappear is a toddler's idea of a right laugh. And watching the mail pop through the hole in the front door? Well, that's a flippin' riot. Nope, I don't get it either. But we don't *need* to get it; we can just use it to create some good old-fashioned entertainment.

SEND YOURSELF A LETTER

GRAB:

- some pencils and paper
- some envelopes
- postage stamps

TO SET UP . . .

1. Leave the pencils and paper out for your child to find them.
2. Have the envelopes and postage stamps nearby.

TO PLAY . . .

1. Explain to your little one that you are going to send a letter to their favourite toy. Get them to draw a picture or make a card. They can practise writing their name, if they like, or just scribbles are great too!
2. While they're busy doing that, write a little card or letter to your child.
3. Put your cards or drawings in envelopes, then write your own address on the front and pop a stamp on them.
4. Go for a walk or a trip to your nearest postbox or post office to post the letters. When they are delivered by the postman to your house, your child's brain will explode with delight!

2+

PLAYING POSTIE

GRAB:

- some soft toys
- a large cardboard box
- scissors
- loads of old birthday or Christmas cards
- some pens, paper and envelopes (optional)
- a bag to use as a 'delivery sack'

TO SET UP . . .

1. Scatter the soft toys around the room.
2. Cut a rectangular hole in the side of the box, like the letter slot in a postbox.
3. Pop all the cards out on the floor with the pens, paper and envelopes (if using).
4. Leave the bag nearby.

TO PLAY . . .

1. Let children post all the cards into the postbox. If they want, they can use the pens, paper and envelopes to make their own and write in them.
2. Then let them empty the postbox and put all the letters into the delivery sack.
3. Finally they can deliver the letters to all the toys around the room.

For little ones: See if the monster can eat the letters of your child's own name in the correct order.

For older ones: Play this with spellings, or with tricky words.

THE LETTER MONSTER

This game is handy because there are so many different ways you could vary it! Below is the version I used with Ewan when he was four and a half and at school, but you could use this to introduce letters to younger ones or even to practise spelling with older ones. If you fancy, you can really go to town with your monster's character. Unleash all those skills your school drama teacher imparted to you! Outta my way, kids!

GRAB:

- an egg box or a box with a hinged lid
- some stick-on googly eyes (optional)
- 5 toys or household items
- a pen and some paper
- scissors

TO SET UP . . .

1. Make your box monster by sticking eyes on the lid. If you don't have googly eyes, make your own with paper or draw some on. Add a tongue too, if you like.

2. Pop the toys or items you've chosen near the monster egg box. For example, when I did this with Ewan, I used a spoon, a book, a teddy, a car and a pencil.

3. Write the letters for each item on paper, then cut them out. For example, I wrote S for spoon, B for book and so on.

4. Then do the same with some other random letters you want your child to know. For example, I used Phase 2 phonics sounds. (For more information about phonics, see page 172.)

5. Lay out the letters next to the monster and the items, then leave it all for your child to find!

TO PLAY . . .

1. Explain to your children that the monster wants to eat the letters of the items he has found. Ask, 'Can you feed the letters to the monster?'

2. Let your child name each item, then find the matching letter. When they get it right, open the monster's mouth and pretend it's chewing the letter up. Yum yum!

3. After all the letters have been eaten, play around with the remaining letters to spell out a name for the monster. (Don't worry if you can only use some of the letters to make a name. Ewan's monster's name was MADINGO.)

4. Feed the monster its name. After that, the monster is so full it does a big burp and all the letters pop out over your kids' heads!

5. Play again! See if they can find more items for the other sounds. Can they make a different name for the monster?

8p

3p

19p

12p

15p

Let your child take turns being the customer and the shopkeeper. It's all brilliant for counting and number recognition!

For older ones: Make the prices more complicated, then get them to work out the correct amount using the coins.

3+

123

THE SHOP

When I was a kid, another child who lived in our street had a toy sweet shop. It had tiny jars with miniature versions of all our favourite sweets, little scales, a till and paper bags. I genuinely thought it was the most magical and wonderful thing I'd ever seen. There is absolutely no doubt in my mind that if you showed that shop to *any* kid today they'd think the same thing. Some things just don't get old, and playing shop is one of them. My two love it. I like to sneak a bit of number learning into it – that way, the five minutes of me playing the role of Miss Rabbit from *Peppa Pig* feel well spent.

GRAB:

- some pens
- Post-its (or bits of paper and Blu-Tack)
- 5 random items
- loads of coins – real or pretend
- a small purse or handbag
- a toy till (if you don't have one, use a box or container)
- shopping bags (optional)

TO SET UP . . .

1. Write five different numbers on five separate Post-its (or bits of paper with Blu-Tack), then stick them to the items – these are your 'price tags'.
2. Pop all the coins into the purse or handbag.
3. Arrange it all with the till so that it looks like a little shop, then wait excitedly for your children to discover it!

TO PLAY . . .

1. Say, 'Welcome to my shop! What would you like to buy?' Then explain to your children that they need to choose an item, then pay for it by giving the shopkeeper the correct number of coins.
2. Once they've selected an item, show them how to read the price tag. If necessary, help them to recognize the number written on it.
3. Then let them count the correct number of coins into your hand. When they have finished counting, double-check the number by counting aloud as you pop the coins into the till. This helps to reinforce the number and the process of counting.
4. If you have a shopping bag, pop the item in it. Then say, 'Bye-bye! Please come back another day.' (And by 'another day' I mean in ten seconds' time!)

In the meantime, cut some letters out yourself and write an anonymous note to your other half. *I know you ate the last of the chocolate*, for example. Useful!

JUNK–MAIL HUNTING

I don't know about you, but we still get free stuff through the door. Newspapers, magazines, even phone books. Those of us with access to, you know, the internet might pop these straight into the recycling bin – but hold it! There is fun to be had first! I can still remember sitting on my grandma's knee while she read the newspaper and pointed to the word 'the', then asked me how many more I could find. I felt an enormous sense of pride when I spotted another 'the' – my first memory of reading. That pride is what I wanted to recreate.

GRAB:

- free post
- some pens (highlighters are good) and paper
- child-friendly scissors
- a glue stick
- some paper

TO SET UP . . .

1. Circle or highlight a few things in the free post.
2. Leave the post open on the table, along with everything else.

TO PLAY . . .

1. Do a letter hunt. Can your little ones find all the letters of their name and highlight or circle them?
2. Ask them to find certain letters. How many can they find? You could even do a tally chart!
3. Get children to spot large letters, then cut them out and stick them on to a bit of paper. This is a great way to practice useful scissor skills at this age when they're just starting school.
4. If your little one is learning tricky words or spellings, get them to make the words using the letters they find.

For little ones:
Start with 1 to 5.

3+

1²₃

THE NUMBER THIEF

Most houses have a pack of playing cards lying around or in a 'random stuff' drawer. They have numbers on them (obviously), so I knew I *must* be able to come up with a simple game using them. Then I remembered one we used to play when I was a teaching assistant in a nursery class. It was shown to me by Mrs Millington, and is a great game for number recognition, number ordering and counting. Ewan was three at the time, and when I tried it out on him it was as popular as it had been in that nursery class!

GRAB:

- a pack of playing cards (if you don't have any, make some with pen and paper)
- play dough or Blu-Tack (optional)
- a small toy

TO SET UP . . .

1. Get the cards out, then line them in order from ace (1) to 10.
2. If you like, use a blob of play dough or Blu-Tack to prop them upright.
3. Sit the toy next to the cards.

TO PLAY . . .

1. Explain that the toy is there to steal a number. It's a naughty number thief!
2. Your child then has to shut their eyes, while you remove one of the cards. Prop it up against the toy so your child can't see what the number is.
3. Tell them they can open their eyes, then ask them to tell you which number is missing. Show them how to count from one in order to discover the missing number.
4. Repeat, with the toy stealing a different number each time.
5. After a few goes, let your child be the thief. You could also take away two or three numbers at a time.

It goes without saying that this game requires adult support and supervision at all times!

DOT-TO-DOT WHODUNNIT

Scissor skills are such a hard thing for tiny fingers to grasp. If you grab a pair of scissors yourself, you'll realize just how complex the set of movements required is – then try to explain it to a child! How any of us learn it is a mystery. Don't worry, though, they all get there in the end. This game is just a fun way to practise, and we all enjoy a little mystery. So, whodunnit?

GRAB:

- a pen and some paper
- 5 different-shaped toys
- some cushions or a container (optional)
- child-friendly scissors

TO SET UP . . .

1. Trace round each of the toys in a dot-to-dot. Use the same number of dots as your little one can confidently recognize. For example, if they are confident counting to five, use five dots and a faint line in between.
2. Hide the toys around the room.
3. Make a little 'jail' out of some cushions or a container (if using).
4. Put the scissors somewhere nearby.

TO PLAY . . .

1. Explain to your children that five of their toys have been very naughty and are on the run – if you like, you can say they've stolen some treats. Your little ones need to find the naughty toys and put them in jail. (Kids just love telling off their toys!)
2. Tell them that the toys have left some clues to help solve the mystery. Can your child join up each dot-to-dot? When they've done that, they need to cut out the shape for their clue.
3. To solve each clue, they need to recognize the toy and find where each toy is hiding. If the dot-to-dot matches, the toy is guilty! It gets sent to the cushion jail (if using). Next, find its accomplices!

For younger children: If they're not ready for letters yet, set them up with their own digger tray anyway and let them explore!

LETTER DIGGERS

Sometimes I get requests from friends who tell me their little ones have no interest in learning the letters of their name. They only want to play with this or that. 'What can I do?' my friends ask. Well, my answer is, 'Just let them play with this or that, and somehow weave the letters in.' In one particular case, 'this and that' were diggers, diggers and more diggers! So my suggestion was to dig for letters. Of course, your child might still show no interest in the letter element of the game, but if that's the case don't worry. Just keep playing. Believe me – it's all slowly being taken on board, without your child even realizing it.

GRAB:

- 2 bits of paper
- a pen
- scissors
- a large tray
- kinetic sand or something to dig in – for example, lentils, porridge oats, etc.
- digger toys

TO SET UP . . .

1. Draw six squares on each bit of paper. Write letters in one set of squares, then cut them out. Leave the other squares blank, and add little tick boxes next to each one.
2. Get the tray and place the cut-out letters in it.
3. Cover the letters with sand. Put the diggers on top.
4. Leave the pen and the bit of paper with the blank boxes next to the digger tray.

TO PLAY . . .

1. Tell children that there are letters hidden under the sand. The diggers need to excavate them!
2. Each time they find a letter, they need to write it in the box and tick it off.
3. Once they have found all six letters, let them hide the letters for you. Or you could also just give them a chocolate biscuit and leave them to play happily with the sand like I did!

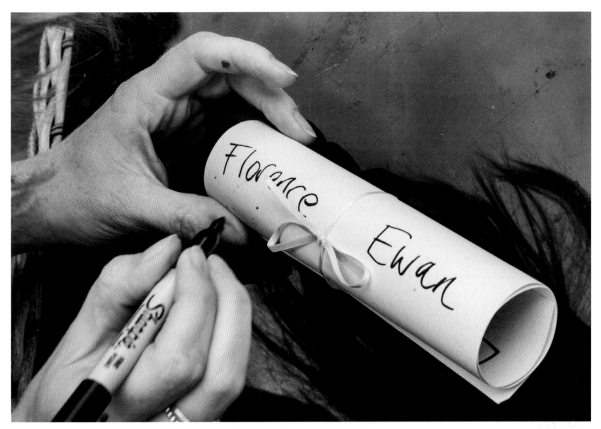

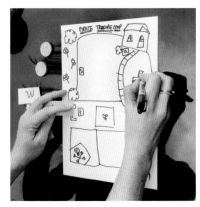

You can vary this game depending on what your child is into. Perhaps a cheeky fairy hid them and left a note? Or maybe it was a disgusting troll, or a naughty witch?

PIRATE TREASURE MAP

'Help! I'm hosting a play date! What can we do?' I get asked this one a lot. Now, I'm lucky, as I have lots of friends with kids the same age as my two, so 'chaos catch-ups' are a regular occurrence. Usually, us adults hide on a sofa with a brew, while the kids slowly destroy every single room in the house. Sometimes, though, I like to throw in a five-minute game to keep them occupied and so I feel like I've done my bit. One hot and sunny day, when Ewan and Florence's besties, Louis and Ollie, came over the kids found that some pirates had also been to visit . . .

GRAB:

- a pen and a bit of paper for each player
- treasure – coins (real or chocolate), buttons or necklaces
- 5 plastic or magnetic letters – if you don't have any, write some on paper and cut them out

TO SET UP . . .

1. Draw a rough map of your house or garden for each child.
2. Hide the letters in different places. Hide the coins in one place – this is your 'treasure'. I buried some gold coins in our sandpit, but you could place a treat under a bucket or a pillow, for example.
3. On the maps, mark the spots where the letters are with a number in a circle, as well as marking the spot where the treasure is with an X.
4. Roll the maps into scrolls, then put kids' names on them. Pop them by the front door, as though they've just come through the letterbox.

TO PLAY . . .

1. Just when the kids are driving you crackers, ask if they just heard something being posted through the door.
2. When they discover the maps, act shocked. Tell them the maps are from Pirate Pete and say, 'He's hidden some treasure! It's your job to follow the map to find all the letters, then write them down. If you do it correctly, you will find the buried treasure!'
3. Help them with where to start, then let them follow the map to find the letters. Remember to write the letters down as they find them.
4. With the fifth letter, they can find the treasure! If they're anything like the four in my garden, they'll be super giddy – and they will have also practised writing five letters. Bingo!

Do a giant version with large numbers, blobs of Blu-Tack and a ball of string. Your child can act as the spider!

SPIDER'S WEB

This game is super simple (my favourite kind of anything). It's also an introduction to number recognition that happened by accident, really. I mainly did this little activity because I didn't want to move my bum off the sofa. I'd just finished writing out my never-ending To Do list, when three-year-old Ewan toddled over and asked what I was up to. 'Do you want to help me make a spider's web?' I asked him. He said he did.

GRAB:

- a pen and some paper

TO SET UP . . .

1. Write consecutive numbers randomly all over the page, then circle them. I did 1 to 20 for Ewan at the time, but you can do however many your little one can confidently attempt.
2. Leave the bit of paper for your child to find.

TO PLAY . . .

1. Ask your little one if they'd like to make a spider's web. If they say yes, show them the piece of paper and ask them to find the first number.
2. Once they've spotted 1, ask, 'What comes next?' When they say 'two', draw a line between 1 and 2.
3. Can they find the next number? Make it seem tricky and funny as your lines criss-cross the page. If they don't know the next number at any point, start counting from one again.
4. Once you've made your web, draw another page of numbers and hand your child the pen. Let them try to join the dots and make the wobbly web.

To make the game a little longer, hide the eggs around the house.

For older ones: You could hide anagrams inside the eggs.

CRACK THE EGG

For some bizarre reason, every child I know seems to like watching those incredibly annoying YouTube videos of other people opening eggs! So I figured why not take that idea and turn it into a wee game? This game can be used for anything: numbers, letters, shapes and colours for very little ones, or tricky spellings for older ones.

GRAB:

- a pen
- 5 bits of paper
- play dough
- tinfoil
- an egg cup
- a teaspoon

TO SET UP . . .

1. On each piece of paper, write down something that you would like your child to work on or learn. When I invented this game for Ewan, it was Phase 2 phonics sounds. (For more on phonics, see page 172.)
2. Fold each bit of paper up as small as you can, then hide it inside a ball of play dough shaped like an egg.
3. Wrap each play-dough egg in tinfoil.
4. Pop one egg in the egg cup on the table, then put the spoon and the remaining eggs alongside it.

TO PLAY . . .

1. Explain to your children that there's something hidden in each egg.
2. Let them open the foil of the egg in the egg cup, then hit it with the teaspoon to 'crack' the egg.
3. What's inside? Do they know? Say whatever is on the paper with them.
4. Repeat with all the eggs.
5. Can they make some eggs for you, writing their own letters, shapes or numbers? Stick the kettle on and leave them to it!

Nonsense words are a useful tool when it comes to using phonics to learn to read! See why on page 173.

You will get rude words. Just sound them out as usual, then dismiss them as silly words!

SILLY SOUP

This is a classroom classic! I feel like I'm letting you in on a teacher secret, as every school I've ever worked in played this game or some version of it. It's a game for what is known as blending in phonics (see page 173) or, in other words, reading. To begin with, some kids find it really difficult to join up letter sounds to make words – for example, when they see 'd-o-g' in a book they might get the letter sounds correct, but then guess the word is 'mum'. It's enough to make you want to face-plant a brick wall. So, maybe put down the book and try this game instead . . .

GRAB:

- 2 different-coloured pieces of paper
- a pen
- scissors
- a large bowl
- a wooden spoon

TO SET UP . . .

1. On one piece of coloured paper, write ten consonants.
2. On the piece of differently coloured paper, write all the vowels.
3. Cut the letters out individually, then fold them up and pop them into the bowl. Put the wooden spoon alongside it.

TO PLAY . . .

1. Explain you're going to make some silly soup. Say, 'Let's see how silly it can be!'
2. Let children mix the letters in the bowl, singing 'Silly soup, silly soup, we're gonna make some silly soup!' Then get them to use the wooden spoon to select one consonant out of the bowl. Next, get them to select a vowel, then another consonant.
3. Ask them to open the letters up. This will reveal a three-letter word known in phonics as a CVC (consonant-vowel-consonant) word.
4. Ask them to sound out the letters. Do they make a real word, or is it a SILLY word?

This is a great game for speech and language without any writing at all. Just pause and let your kids choose what's going to happen next!

3+

abc

'TELL ME A STORY FROM YOUR HEAD'

Has your little one ever asked you this? My nan had an endless bank of stories about an imaginary underground mole world that she'd describe to us as we skipped over molehills on our way home. Crazy Nanny (as my kids call her!) now tells my children stories about fairies and moles, and they get as much joy out of it as I did. And I've found a way to get reading into their adventures, as well!

GRAB:

- something to write on – a Magna Doodle, a blackboard, a whiteboard, some chalk on a blank wall, or pens and paper
- your imagination!

TO SET UP . . .

1. Have whatever you are going to write on somewhere close to you.

TO PLAY . . .

1. Ask children if they'd like to hear a story. As you tell the story, stop when you get to a part with a consonant-vowel-consonant (CVC) word (or a simple word) and write the word instead of saying it. To mix it up, let your kids choose parts of the story too.

Here are some examples:

Say, 'One morning, I woke up and got some cereal from a . . .' then write BOX.
Say, 'Then I put on my trousers and my . . .' and write TOP.
Say, 'Then I went to the . . .' and write PARK, then say, 'with my lovely fluffy . . .' and write DOG.
Say, 'Suddenly I saw a . . .' This time let children choose what you saw. Mine said a ghost!
Say, 'The ghost said . . .' and write BOO.
Say, 'Which made the dog do a terrified . . .' and write POO.
Say, 'And the ghost said "Yuck," and flew away again' and write THE END.

WTAF IS PHONICS?

So perhaps you're the parent of a little one and were naturally expecting your child to learn about Annie Apple and Clever Cat just like you did as a kid (any other 80s/90s kids out there?). Then you hear the word PHONICS. Nursery says, 'We're starting phonics,' to your three-year-old, and I can almost guarantee you'll be thinking, *WTAF is phonics?* But you won't want to admit this to the enthusiastic teacher, so instead you just smile, nod and then go home, silently panicking.

But don't panic. I can explain it in five minutes (way less actually – it's really simple!), and I also did a short series of videos on my YouTube channel if you prefer to watch me chat about it instead.

GET RID OF THE 'UH'

When it comes to learning to read, nurseries and schools don't start with ABC any more. Instead they teach the SOUNDS the letters make, which is all 'phonics' means (*phon* is *sound* in Greek). This makes it much easier for children to match the letters they see to the actual sounds we hear in a word.

So instead of saying 'suh' or 'ess' for *s*, they learn 'sssssss' (hiss like a snake). Then when your child reads the word *sit* they sound out 'sssssss-i-t' as opposed to 'suh-i-t' which would sound like 'suhit' – no such word (no shuit!). I use the example of the word *mop* in my videos. Saying *m* is 'muh' and *p* is 'puh' means that when the children see the word 'mop' they would say 'muhopuh' – again, no such word. So in phonics the sound for *m* is 'mmmm' and the sound for *p* is a very short, soft 'p' like a little pop noise. Mmmm-o-p. Much better.

Doing it this way means that kids can quickly start to 'blend' the letter sounds together to make a word and therefore read much sooner. Because they can hear themselves saying the word as they form the sounds for each letter, they get clues, which help their little brains connect the two. This is why the very first bit of phonics is simply playing listening games.

LET'S GET STARTED

The listening games in phonics are what is known as Phase 1. There are six phases in total where kids gradually (over many weeks) learn more and more letters in a specific order that someone much cleverer than me has designed.

After playing listening games, the first sounds that phonics introduces your children to are:

SATPIN

If you want to try these at home, then it will match what your nursery or school does. However, I have always found children to be self-absorbed little beings, so when I introduce letters through play I usually start with the letters in their name. I began by setting up games like Target Practice (page 63) or Letter Racetrack (page 75).

DID SOMEONE MENTION DIGRAPHS?

Once kids have learned single letter sounds (Phase 2), they move on to learning the sounds that two letters make when they are together in a word. These letter pairs are called **DIGRAPHS** (because we all love a technical word that confuses us, right?).

Learning digraphs starts simply. For example, kids learn that when we see *ck* in a word we don't make a sound for each letter; instead, we simply say both letters together as one sound. So *kick* isn't pronounced 'k-i-c-kuh', because the *c* and the *k* go together to make one sound. You still with me?

As they move through the phases they'll learn other digraphs like *ur*, *oi*, *ar* and so on. By learning the particular sounds that certain pairs of letters make, kids can easily read words like *turn*, *coin* and *far* – all they do is spot the digraph they know, then make the correct sound for it. T-ur-n. C-oi-n. F-ar. Easy!

Eventually, just as you think you're getting the hang of the jargon, the kids will start learning **SPLIT DIGRAPHS**. These are still digraphs – two letters making one sound – but this time the two letters making that sound are split up in the word. The word *made* is a good example: together the *a–e* makes the 'ay' sound, but the letters are split up by the *d*. Have I lost you? This is what replaced the old-fashioned 'magic E', if you remember that.

BLENDING AND SEGMENTING

With phonics, from very early on kids will be able to blend the sounds they have learned to read words. They start with what are called CVC words, which are simply any words that go consonant–vowel–consonant. For example, *cat*, *sit*, *dug*. They will play with words that make no sense too, for example *mip*, *vop* and *lat*, because this enables them to practise blending techniques on their own without having to memorize the meaning of the words too. (See my game Silly Soup on page 169 for a fun way to do this.)

If a child sees a word on paper that they don't know how to read, they can chop it up into the sounds they recognize. This is called 'segmenting'. (Yes, like an orange. Don't ask me why.) Once they've segmented a word into sounds, they can then use those sounds to help them read the word. When they start writing, they can even use this process to help with spelling.

THE BASICS ARE ENOUGH!

It's not crucial for you to understand phonics and all its technical jargon in its entirety. There are wonderful teachers out there to teach this to your children. You can figure it all out at the same time as your child – and, if you're having trouble, just ask the kids to talk you through it! Doing this shows that you're supporting them while also providing a confidence boost when they patiently and proudly explain* what a digraph is to you. In the meantime, if you're playing ANY kind of letter or alphabet game with your children, HOWEVER you are doing it, you're a blinkin' GREAT parent. End of.

*That, or patronizingly ask, 'You mean you don't know?' before gleefully singing, 'Mummy doesn't know what sound "ea" makes!' Cheers, kiddo.

PHONICS ISN'T EVERYTHING!

While playing, I often use both the letter names (alphabet) and sounds (phonics) when explaining letters to my kids. The reason I do this is because of Ewan's name. If I told him the *E* in his name is an 'eh' (as per phonics) then it's rather confusing that it makes a 'yew' sound in his name. So instead I always say it's an 'Eeee' because it is – no adult spells their name over the phone as 'Duh, ah, i, sssssss, yuh' – madness! In phonics we initially learn that *ch* makes a 'chuh' sound – but what would Christopher think? Or Charlotte?

This is why I use both the letter names and their sounds in my videos. For me, it's like telling children that a cat is called a cat but it goes 'meow'. If kids can grasp that, then they can easily understand that an 'en' (*n*) makes a 'nnn' sound.

Phonics isn't the be all and end all when it comes to learning to read. There are many exceptions to the sounds, because the English language is flipping complicated and confusing. I think it's useful for kids to know both the letter names and the sounds they can make from the very beginning to help explain these exceptions later on. Be honest with them about how tricky it can be (for example, words like *knight*, *circle*, *great*), and just explain exceptions as simply as you can. Don't forget, though, that your kids' teachers are always there too and you can talk to them if you want advice about phonics.

There are plenty of words that can't be sounded out. These are called 'tricky words' and just need to be learned by memory. Some examples are *we*, *go*, *what* and *they*. You can find lists online.

All the phonics sounds can be found easily online by typing 'Jolly Phonics' into YouTube.

When three letters combine to make one sound, it's called a trigraph. For example, the *igh* in the word *light*. Excellent – more complicated jargon!

A good time to start teaching your own kids phonics is when school or nursery does, and you can provide support from home. Be led by your child as well. When they start to show an interest, that's your cue to crack out some letter-learning fun!

Upper-case or lower-case letters? Introduce both, but use lower-case letters more frequently as we see more of them when we read.

Just knowing the basics is plenty. I promise. You don't need to know all the terminology teachers use.

'High-frequency words' are just words we see loads, so they are good ones for kids to know by heart.

If you want to know what all six phonics phases are, pop to my website fiveminutemum.com/2018/06/15/wtaf-is-phonics/

made

An example of a split digraph:

a_e

makes the 'ay' sound

5

QUICK IDEAS FOR . . .

ABOUT TIME

FIVE MINUTES' PEACE
TINY ONES
RAINY DAYS
BOX GAMES
SPRING DAYS
MARK—MAKING
MESSY PLAY
SUNNY DAYS
SPLASHY PLAY
AUTUMN DAYS
HENRY AND HIS CF WARRIOR BUDDIES
THE TERRIBLE TWOS
COLOURS
ON THE BEACH
SHAPES AND BLOCKS
ENJOYING NATURE
MAGNETIC LETTERS AND NUMBERS
CHRISTMAS

ABOUT TIME

After I had children, it suddenly seemed as though time had started following a new, mad set of rules. During the BC (before children) era time just ticked away according to the clock on the wall, but AC (after ch– OK, you get it!) time was apparently either set to warp speed or at a complete standstill. Some days, my toddler would disappear in the direction of the bathroom while I was stuck on the sofa feeding the baby, and I would soon hear the toilet roll being unwound at a rate of knots and the taps going on and off. I would then lose an hour attempting to clean up the mess, while simultaneously trying to burp the fussing baby, then: 'Oh FFS! **WE'RE LATE FOR PLAYGROUP . . . AGAIN.**'

Other days, I'd be feeding the same baby on the same sofa with the same toddler at my knees, but there'd still be an hour to go before playgroup started. It'd be too early for another snack, we'd have already watched an hour of inane kids' shows, and I would be desperate for another adult to speak to. I would be **BORED**.

It's a truth commonly acknowledged (by everyone except the knobby 'treasure every moment' brigade) that we can love and enjoy our kids at the same time as sometimes finding parenting difficult, boring and lonely. None of these emotions are mutually exclusive – in fact, we can switch between feeling grateful and feeling bored in a matter of seconds, and *that* there is what brings on the guilt. Ah, the guilt. A big fat, fresh dollop of the stuff. To my mind, if you find yourself feeling guilty it's actual, real-life proof that you're a good parent. You're worrying about your child and how you can do better for them, right? GOOD PERSON. (That's what I tell myself, anyway.)

What we really need to do, though, is to kick that guilt into touch. Truly get rid of it. Free ourselves. And I have **JUST** the thing:

QUICK IDEAS!

In this chapter, you'll find all the ideas I put to use during moments of guilt. I use these grab-and-go ideas over and over, and they're all simple to set up. They'll keep the kids occupied enough to free me up, or they'll give us something to do together to make the slow days pass quicker. They are especially good for the wee ones from age one upwards. This is the stuff I did when my bairns were tiny and I needed to keep them busy at my feet while I cooked dinner or cleaned the bathroom. Before I do jobs, I like to play with the kids for five minutes – that way, I have no qualms about shooing them off afterwards and saying, 'Go and play.' They've had some quality time with me. Now to encourage independent discovery. My conscience is clear.

It was after writing down all these quick ideas here that I realized just how many there are! I have **MY OWN MUM** to credit for this. She's the queen of speedy, easy fun for children. It's only as I watch her set up activities for my own lucky kids that I realize exactly why my childhood was such a happy one and why I was probably always destined to become Five Minute Mum . . .

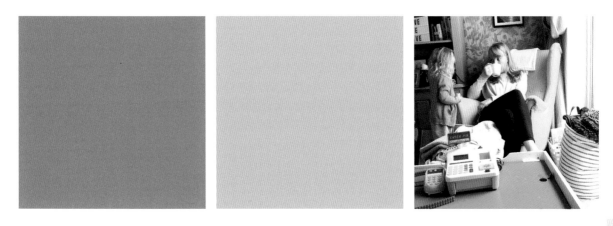

Have a sort—out of your kids' toys. Tidying things up always makes children want to play with their toys again. As annoying as it might be to put things back where they belong, doing it every so often is ALWAYS worth it for the peace it brings afterwards. You can even turn it into a game with your little ones to see who can put toys away the fastest!

FIVE MINUTES' PEACE

Ah, peace. That thing we all crave from the moment our little human first goes 'wah!' On bended knee, we beg, 'Please, just give me five minutes, kids.' Well, I hope these ideas might just give it to you – and, if you're lucky, maybe a wee bit longer. So, pick an activity, then quick! Run to the loo! Write an email! Put the kettle on! GO!

1. A 'REAL' HANDBAG

Grab an old handbag and purse – if you don't have one lying around, charity shops are a good place to look. If your child is old enough to avoid choking, fill the purse with real coins, then put it in the handbag. Throw in things like old travel tickets or cards, expired bank cards, old keys on keyrings, and any other bits and bobs that will make it seem like a grown-up's handbag. Then let your child find it and explore it!

2. TAT BOX

A huge favourite! You know the plastic tat you get in party bags, on the front of magazines or from fast-food meals? The stuff that gets played with for thirty seconds then thrown out? Well, how about collecting it in a shoebox? Get a box for each child, and keep them out of reach. Next time you pick up a bit of tat, instead of binning it, chuck it in the tat box. Then, one day when you're at home and want five minutes, pull the tat box out. The kids will think all their Christmases have come at once!

3. TEDDY ZIP WIRE

Grab a bit of string, then tie one end to something high (such as the stairwell bannister) and the other end to something down low and near to the ground. Get one of those small clothes hangers with clips attached, or just put pegs on a standard hanger. Gather a bunch of teddies, then let the kids clip them on to the hanger and send them down the zip wire. Whee! Up and down the teddies go! I like to sit and watch from a distance with a cuppa.

4. WATER BOWL

I know, this sounds messy, right? It's not if you do what I do, and fill a washing-up bowl with water then plonk it in the base of the shower or the empty bath. That way the kids can splash all they like and there's no mess to clean up! Pop in a load of random items – scoops, a tea set, jugs – and leave your little ones to amuse themselves pouring water. Meanwhile, you can sit next to them texting your friends to see who's free for a coffee. Anyone? Please?

5. PHOTO SHOOT

Set up the camera on your phone for your children, then tell them to go and take pictures of all their favourite toys. (If you have an iPhone, a handy tip is to go to your settings and turn on 'guided access' first. This locks the device on a single app, meaning your kids won't be able to send random emails or accidentally buy six pairs of shoes.) Meanwhile, you can sit back in total peace. Bliss.

Toddlers aged between one and two love those lift-the-flap books. Make your own, using an ordinary book and some Post-its!

TINY ONES

It can sometimes be tricky to think up fun things to do with very little ones who are aged between one and two. I wasn't particularly creative when my kids were this age (sleep deprivation stole my brain cells), but these are some of the activities we enjoyed when I did have a spark of energy (thanks to copious amounts of caffeine).

1. HIDE THE TOY

Get three cups (or buckets or bowls), then hide a small toy underneath each. Lift the cups one at a time to reveal the toys to your bub. Then move the cups around, and see if your little one can find each toy again. When they get bored, sit the toys on top of the cups, then grab a ball. See if your little one can knock the toys off by throwing or kicking the ball. (If you don't have a ball, a bit of screwed-up tinfoil also works!)

2. PHOTO PUZZLES

Do you have random photos lying around the house that you haven't got around to framing yet? Or maybe you printed 100 so you could get 20 per cent off, and you've still got the extras? Me too. So chop them up and make them into 'puzzles'! For very little ones, just cut the photos in half along a wavy line, then once they've put a photo back together, talk about who is in it. As your child grows more confident, you can chop the photos into more bits. At this early age kids love to see familiar faces, so this is the perfect way to practise names with lots of brilliant chatter.

3. SOFA TUNNELS AND FORTS

A classic! Make a tunnel for your baby to crawl through by putting a sofa cushion between a coffee table and a chair, or over two chairs. You can also make a fort at one end, if you like. I once made a tunnel all the way round our lounge, then gave the kids a soft ball to push through it.

4. PASTA POST

One of my blog faves. Get any small cardboard box and punch small holes all over it. Then fill a pot with dry pasta (use something chunky like penne rather than spaghetti) and give it to your little one to 'post' through the holes. Very good for five minutes' peace! (Note that some kids, especially little ones, will obviously try to eat the dry pasta, so make sure you watch them like a hawk.)

5. BALLOONS

I always keep a packet of balloons in my 'odds and ends' drawer for boring days or birthdays. If you have some handy, blow up a few and draw funny faces on them. Then let your little one bat the balloons around with their hands and try to catch them. If you want to, give your kids a paper or plastic plate to use as a bat.

RAINY DAYS

Oh, those rainy days. We live in the north-west of England, and up here that's basically ALL days – hence why there are quite a few of these ideas! Pissing it doon again? See if one of these will help to stave off the wall-climbing for another hour . . .

1. PUZZLE GIFT BAGS

Grab a puzzle, then wrap the pieces in bits of newspaper. Chuck them in a gift bag, then give it to your kids. They get to unwrap the 'presents', then make the puzzle. And who doesn't love a present?

2. LIVING-ROOM RUGBY

Grab a bit of ribbon or string and tuck it into the back of your trousers so the end is hanging out. Do the same to your child. Choose a large space, preferably with a soft floor that you can kneel on comfortably – we do this in the living room. Explain to your children that the game is to try to pull out the other player's ribbon, while also stopping your opponent from grabbing yours. Start off facing each other, then say, 'Ready . . . steady . . . go!' After they've had enough, pop a large sofa cushion in front of you, then let the kids have a go at running and 'tackling' you to the floor – great for burning off some of that 'cooped up indoors all day' energy.

3. NURSERY RHYME BASH-ALONG

If your kids have some musical instruments, get them out. If not, grab anything from the kitchen that they can 'play' (bash) – a saucepan and wooden spoon is always a winner. Pick five nursery rhymes, then sing them together and play along. Take turns playing each of the 'instruments', and let your kids suggest favourite songs to sing.

4. PUZZLE HUNT

Get a puzzle and hide all the pieces around a room. Can your kids find all the pieces then complete the puzzle? For older ones, set a timer and get them to see how quickly they can do it!

5. STICKY STORYBOARD

String a bit of masking tape up between two chairs, with the sticky side facing towards you. Grab some Post-its (or some bits of paper) and a pen. You can draw pictures to tell a story, then stick them up on the line in order. Can your kids line up the letters of their name in the right order? Maybe they can even write the letters themselves, then stick their name on to the line?

Don't forget, of course, that a rainy day also means you can get on your wellies and raincoat, grab your umbrella, and head outside to splash in big old puddles. Pure joy! Plus, afterwards you get to come home, have a hot chocolate and snuggle under the blanket with a movie on.

6. TRACING TOYS 3+

Ask your children to go and choose three of their favourite toys. Can they draw round each one? Use chalk on the ground, or pencils on paper. You could even make a trail round the toys out of stones or pom-poms!

7. BIRTHDAY CANDLES 2+

Grab a blob of play dough or some leftover dough from baking, some empty cupcake cases and some birthday candles. Then get your kids to 'make cakes' and stick candles in the top of each one. It always amazes me how long my kids will do this for.

8. MAKE IT DARK! 1+

Shut the curtains. Turn the lights out. My kids love the excitement of making it dark. Give them a torch and read a book in the dark. You could even give them glow sticks and have a disco!

9. MASKING TAPE 1+

My go-to item! I always have a roll on hand, as it means I can instantly create some fun. You could tape your kids' names out on the floor, then let them peel each letter off. Another idea is to rip off ten long pieces of tape, then give it to your kids to make a track or a road. You can use it as plasters on poorly teddies at the 'hospital', or to mark out a trail to follow, or to make numbers to hop along. You can let your kids draw on it. Masking tape is fantastic for so many games.

10. CUSHION STEPPING STONES 2+

Lay a load of cushions in a trail across the floor, then tell your kids that they have to get from one bit of furniture to another without touching the LAVA! (By which I mean the carpet or the floor.) Make different paths. This might not be one for the house-proud but with a three- and a five-year-old I'm beyond caring! (This one's like The Trap on page 77 but without the learning bit.)

As a treat, pop a cushion in a big box and let your kids have a 'box picnic'. This also contains all the mess, so you can just tip the crumbs outside afterwards!

BOX GAMES

A cardboard box is one of life's greatest gifts to anyone caring for a child, and in this age of online ordering I find they are plentiful in our house. Below are some of the things we've done with boxes. (Of course, you can also just lob one at your kids and let their imaginations run wild!)

1. JUNK ROBOT 3+

Grab a big box, then get a load of random bits and bobs out of the recycling bin – small boxes, bottle tops, plastic bottles, bits of foil, etc. Then put it all together to create a robot! Use masking tape to stick things on. If you have stickers, use them to make controls and buttons. Great fun if you also cut holes for a person's head and arms in the big box, then let your little one become the robot!

2. BOX SLEDGE 2+

Poke two small holes in one side of a big box, then tie a bit of rope or string through the holes to turn the box into a sledge. Sit the kids in it, then pull them along a hard floor. After that, let them have a turn pulling their toys around in it.

3. RAMP RACE 2+

Flatten out a big box by cutting through one edge, then write START and FINISH at either end. Set it up as a ramp off a sofa or chair, then race toy cars or trains down it. Who will win?

4. TORCH FORT 1+

Turn a big box on its side and throw a blanket over the top. Ta-da! Instant fort! Give your kids a torch, then let them hide in the fort and make shapes on the walls or read a story.

5. GUESS THE TOY 3+

Cut a hole in one side of a box that's just big enough to fit a child's arm through it. Then put five toys inside the box and close the top. Get your little ones to poke their arm inside and describe what they feel. Can they guess which toy is which?

Sometimes going to the same old park gets quite boring. Take pegs and clip them on to different leaves to make 'natural paintbrushes'. It's also great fun to roll toy cars down slides or push teddies on swings, and a bucket and spade is good for digging in mud.

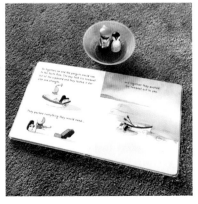

SPRING DAYS

These games can be played both indoors and outdoors, so they're perfect for the changeable spring weather. You can take them outside to a park or the garden, but if you need to be in during a downpour, no worries. I always love it when spring comes back around and we can finally breathe some fresh air on a daily basis again!

1. HALF STICKERS

In our house, stickers seem to multiply. We always have random pages of them knocking around. I often snip the stickers in half, then let the kids match them up again. Sometimes I put the halves on a bit of paper. Other times, I hide them around the house or the garden. Don't forget to peel the page backing off first to make it easier for little hands to peel stickers off themselves.

2. GUESS THE SOUND

Grab five things that make noise – you can use musical instruments or bits and bobs from around the house. Show your little one all the items. Ask them to turn round so they can't see you, then 'play' one of the items. Can they guess which one it was? You can also play this game outside, sitting on a blanket, and afterwards listen to and talk about the other sounds you can hear around you. Are there birds tweeting? Planes flying overhead? Dogs barking?

3. OAT CUPCAKES

Grab some oats and some empty cupcake cases. Write numbers inside the cases, then get your little one to spoon the correct number of spoonfuls of oats into the cases. If you do this in the garden the birds can eat the spilled oats. If you do it indoors, lay out a blanket and shake it outside for the birds afterwards.

4. BRING A BOOK TO LIFE

Have a look at your books, and pick one that tells a simple story you can easily bring to life with a few small props. We have one that's about a boy and a penguin in a boat, so I grabbed a small toy figure, a toy penguin and a plastic bowl to use as the boat. Then we read the story together, and acted it out with our props. We sailed them out of the house, round the garden and back again. Perhaps your character rings the doorbell or goes up for a bath? Take the book along with you as you go!

5. MEASURING TAPE

A retractable measuring tape, if you have one, can make for some great fun! This is an activity for the older ones, as measuring tapes can be a bit tricky and you need to be careful with them. (For smaller ones, a soft fabric or plastic tape will do just as well.) They're wonderful for measuring everything around the house, and for counting beyond twenty. What's the biggest thing your kids can find to measure?

When your little one does a lovely scribbly drawing, keep it somewhere safe. Then, when a special event comes up and you need a gift card, just cut a heart shape out of the scribble. Stick the scribble heart on to another bit of card and boom! You've got a gorgeous handmade card, and you haven't even had to bribe your kids to 'make a card for Granny, *please*?'

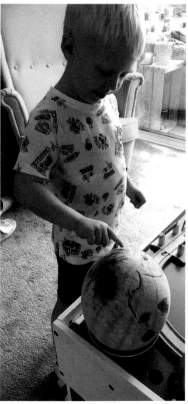

MARK—MAKING

This is useful teacherspeak for writing or drawing. Mark-making is a precursor to writing, so it's a useful thing to encourage. Some kids have no interest in putting a pen on paper – Ewan certainly didn't until he started school – so finding other ways to invite them to make marks is a good way to go.

1. USE TOY CARS 2+

Larger toy cars are best for this – the chunky kind. Tape a pen to the back of each car so the nib is pointing down and will make contact with paper. (Any pen will do, but it might be easier to use a chunky felt-tip one.) Then put the cars on a big bit of paper and let your child drive them around to make tracks. Do any of the shapes happen to look like numbers or letters? If so, point it out to your little one.

2. DO IT UPSIDE DOWN 2+

Tape a bit of paper under a low table or a chair, then leave a box of crayons and a cushion next to it. When your child discovers these things, they can lie down and make an upside-down picture!

3. GET FUNKY 2+

Let your little one draw on some unusual things! They could use a biro on a banana skin, some chalk on tree bark, or a pen on some leaves. You could even tape some newspaper to a window or across the floor, then let them draw on it.

4. DRAWING WITHOUT PAPER 1+

Oh, balls! Nothing to draw on? Unroll some kitchen paper or a loo roll and draw on that! If you're up for getting messy, it's also fun to make watery paint then draw lightly with fingers and let it seep into the tissue.

5. FREEZE A WATERMELON 2+

Yep, you read that right. I froze a watermelon! It was an accident, but when I took it out of the freezer the water made a constant frost on the outside, and my kids ended up drawing and writing on it with their fingers for AGES.

Strip your kids naked and get them to do these ones outside if at all possible. Otherwise, those charity collection bags you get through the door or bin liners make excellent little aprons.

MESSY PLAY

'Argh! Oh god, no! Anything but messy!' That's what this usually makes me say too. But sometimes – just sometimes – I'm in the mood to let my kids 'get creative' and I design a disaster zone so thorough that I have to shut off that area of the house for the rest of the day.

1. BUBBLE PAINTING 3+

Another nursery-classroom classic! Pop equal amounts of non-toxic paint and liquid soap into a cup, then add a splash of water. Grab a straw and some paper. Let your kids blow bubbles in the paint mixture with the straw, then catch the bubbles on the paper to make beautiful patterns. Just don't leave the kids unattended with this one – I did with Ewan once, and I returned to an Oompa Loompa!

2. YOGHURT 1+

If you've got a little baby who eats everything (like Flo did!), letting them try painting or play dough can be difficult. Instead, use natural yoghurt tipped on to a tray and add some dots of natural food colouring, then let your bub swirl it around to their heart's content – and they can lick it all they like!

3. SHAVING FOAM 2+

This is my go-to for messy play. With a cheap can of shaving foam, you can make paint for the bath by adding food colouring to some foam in a plastic bowl, mixing it up with a paintbrush. You can also spray it on a door outside, then give your kids a paintbrush to make marks in it. If you're feeling crackers, spray some foam on a tray, then sprinkle (eco-friendly) glitter on it and let them go nuts. (You'll be finding glitter forevermore, mind.)

4. POTIONS 2+

Save used plastic bottles, soap pumps, formula or washing-powder canisters (the ones that come with those scoops) and medicine syringes. Rinse everything out, then fill each container with some water and pop a splash of different food colouring in each one. Let your kids mix the different-coloured liquids up to make a potion!

5. STONE PAINTING 2+

This is good if you want to get some fresh air before you crack on with the messy stuff. Go for a little walk and collect a few stones. Then come home and get the paints out. Nice and simple – the best stuff always is.

If you want to encourage green fingers in little ones, a great place to start is by growing sunflowers, or by popping mustard cress seeds on a damp piece of cotton wool in an empty eggshell.

SUNNY DAYS

The BEST kind of days! If we can be out in the garden, I am happy. I'm quite green-fingered, so anything that keeps the kids busy while I garden in peace is right up my street.

1. WATER PAINTING

An absolute fave! Give the kids a bucket of water and a paintbrush, then let them 'paint' the shed, fence, walls, floor – anything they like. This also works well on cardboard.

2. CHALK CLEAN-UP

If you have an empty spray bottle, fill it with water. Make chalk marks on walls or fences, then let your little one clean them up using the spray bottle. If you want some learning fun in there, write letters or numbers and shout each one out as your child erases it.

3. SHADOW TRACING

Get some chalk to draw on a wall or the ground, or use a big roll of paper and some pens. Take it in turns to make shapes with your body, then trace round the shadows you create.

4. CAR WASH

If your little one has an outdoor toy car or trike, or a playhouse or slide, give them a bucket filled with plenty of soapy bubbles and tell them it's time to give everything a clean. Give them a selection of sponges, brushes and cloths to use. Kids are surprisingly happy to do this!

5. SMASHING ICE

Grab some cups and fill them with water, then pop in some plastic toys, letters, numbers, ribbons or coins – whatever you like that is appropriate for the age of your little one. Then into the freezer they go! When you're making your Friday G & T (not just me, surely?), take them out and give the kids toy hammers or spoons to bash the ice and free the items. Ah, cheers!

Bath toys can get a bit mucky – which is a bit random, really, as they get 'cleaned' every night! I load ours into the dishwasher to clean them and save myself a lot of time.

SPLASHY PLAY

I once heard someone say, 'If in doubt, add water', and I find this applies to quite a lot of life. I spent much of my pregnancy in the bath or a swimming pool, and my two are proper little water babies. Thankfully we don't always need to go through the ball-ache of putting swimwear on children to have fun with the wet stuff.

1. WATER MAZE 3+

This is another one of Henry's games. (See pages 105 and 203 for more blow-tastic fun!) Grab a tray with sides that are at least a couple of centimetres high, then put some water in it. Use blocks or Duplo to create a simple maze, and put a ping-pong ball or plastic bottle top at the start of the maze. Leave some straws nearby. Your kids then use a straw to blow the ball round the maze.

2. SQUIRT 2+

Use squirting bath toys or, if you don't have them, some clean empty medicine dispenser syringes (Calpol), and squirt letters and numbers off the bath or bath tiles. I stick foam letters and numbers (which can be bought in all supermarkets) to the wall, and the kids have to squirt the one I've shouted until it falls into the bath. Sometimes we race to see who can squirt them fastest.

3. DISCO BATH 1+

Pop some glow sticks into the bath and switch the lights out. Play a bit of music and have a mini rave-up in the water. Big fish, little fish, cardboard box hand actions to accompany, obviously!

4. WASHING UP 2+

This one's good if you've got jobs to do in the kitchen. Let your kids stand at the sink – I use two or three chairs so they're nice and safe. Put the washing-up bowl in the sink, then turn the cold tap on so it's running very slowly into the bowl. Give your kids all the plastic cups and bowls and ask them to 'wash up'.

5. SINK OR FLOAT? 3+

A little science experiment! Get a clear container and fill it with water – I use an empty plastic milk bottle. Gather five different waterproof items from around the house. Hold one item up, and ask your child, 'Do you think this will sink to the bottom or float on the top?' Then drop the item in and see what happens! Sort the items into two piles: those that sink, and those that float. Chat about why each one does what, if you want to.

During autumn, we go to our favourite park and take family photos. It's so nice to compare year on year, and the autumn light makes for beautiful pictures.

AUTUMN DAYS

My favourite season! As a kid, my brother and I used to love collecting conkers. We once completely filled his newspaper-delivery bag and then couldn't carry it home. We conducted all sorts of experiments to try to make our conkers rock-hard so we could win a conker match. (This obsession probably explains why the first three ideas here are for what to do with conkers once you've collected hundreds of the things . . .)

1. CONKER TUNNELS 3+ 💬

Get a cardboard box and cut out five small semicircles along one bottom edge to make tunnel holes. Write numbers above each tunnel based on your little one's ability. Roll or hit the conkers through the tunnels. Can you get all five?

2. CONKER RACES 3+ ✒️

Choose your racing conker, then decorate it with paint or nail varnish. Make a ramp – a cardboard box works, or you can also use a large sofa cushion. Lean your ramp against the sofa or another piece of furniture, then race your conkers down it. The player who is the first to win five times is the ultimate champion!

3. CONKER LETTER AND NUMBER GAMES 3+ abc

Use a marker pen to write numbers and letters on the pale part of each conker, then you can use them to play all sorts of games, such as The Number Thief (page 157) or Treasure Hunt (page 61). You can even pop them in a container filled with water, then see if your child can scoop out the letters of their name using a spoon.

4. PUMPKIN AND SUNFLOWER SEEDS 2+ 1²3

If you had sunflowers in your garden over summer, you'll be left with big flower heads full of seeds in early autumn. Put the flower heads on a tray then let your wee ones try to get the seeds out! Likewise, if you carve a pumpkin for Halloween, scoop the mulchy innards on to a tray. Then give your kids some spoons and a muffin tray, and let them explore the texture and make 'cakes'. Be sure to watch them, to make sure they don't try to eat the seeds or pumpkin.

5. WRITE ON A PUMPKIN 3+ ✒️

The surface of a pumpkin happens to be excellent for mark-making! Draw all over it with a whiteboard pen. You can design all kinds of funny faces, or play Rub It Out (page 71). At Halloween, I often buy a couple of extra smaller pumpkins specifically for this.

If you can, get hold of some bendy reusable straws. Being able to bend them at all angles makes the games easier, and also sillier – and being silly is always a desired outcome!

This bunny is an Easter version of 'Return Rudolf's Nose' on page 217 – another great blowing game!

HENRY AND HIS CF WARRIOR BUDDIES

As you already know from Blow Football (page 105), Henry is my cousin's little boy who has cystic fibrosis. These quick ideas are all designed to make his physiotherapy, which involves blowing exercises, a little bit more exciting. And, of course, they're fun for everyone to play! There's something about blowing that brings out the giggles in all of us.

1. BALL RACES 2+ 123

Tip a cardboard box on to its side on the floor so that the opening is facing you – this is your 'goal'. Screw up five small bits of paper per player – leftover wrapping paper is ideal for this. Give each player a straw and explain that, when you say 'Go!', they have to blow their bits of paper into the goal one at a time. The first player to get all five of their bits of paper in the goal is the winner.

2. CUP ROCKETS 3+

This is a good one if you have leftover paper or plastic cups from a party. Each player gets a cup and turns it into a rocket by decorating it or drawing on it. Next, get two lengths of sellotape, one a few centimetres longer than the other. With the sticky sides facing, stick the shorter piece along the middle of the longer piece, so that the two ends remain sticky. Then stick both ends to the side of a cup rocket, so the tape is like a big cup handle. Thread a long piece of string through the handle, so the cup hangs from the string. Tie the string across a room. Now you're ready to play! Have rocket races by blowing your cup along the string.

3. BALLOON RACE 2+

Use masking tape to make a line on the floor at one end of a room, then write FINISH on it. At the other end of the room, have an inflated balloon waiting for each player. Players have to blow their balloon across the room, and the first to cross the finishing line wins!

4. CAT AND MOUSE 2+

Give one player a ball of cotton wool – they are the mouse. Give another player a paper or plastic cup – they are the cat. The mouse blows the cotton wool around on the floor, randomly and as quickly as they can, while the cat tries to catch it with the cup. If this is too easy for the cat, stick a piece of string to the bottom of their cup so they need to hold the string and drop the cup on the mouse to catch it.

5. SNOOKER 2+ 123

Tape six paper or plastic cups round the edge of a table, like the pockets on a snooker table. Get two rolled-up bits of tinfoil and a straw per player. You can use an elastic band (or a few) round the ball to differentiate the balls. Start with the tinfoil 'balls' at one end of the table. Players take turns to use their straws to blow their balls, and either try to score by getting a ball into a pocket or use their balls to block other players' balls. One blow counts as one turn. If another player knocks one of your balls into a pocket, that counts as a score for you. When you get a ball in a pocket, your ball goes back to the starting end of the table.

I keep old towels in a box downstairs, as they are so useful for kids this age – potty training, cleaning up messes or drying them off after water play. All hail the old towel!

THE TERRIBLE TWOS

This is a fun phase, isn't it? Two-year-olds can't quite communicate their exact needs yet, but they are desperate to exert their opinions. The frustrated result is often a screaming, tight-fisted, kicky meltdown. Lovely. Once, red-faced and with steam coming out of my ears, I had to carry Ewan out of a supermarket like a rugby ball. We've all been there. Being patient, staying calm and riding it out seems to work most of the time – but sometimes distraction works really nicely too! So, with Flo, I set up these little activities in preparation of the moments when I'd need to speedily intercept an imminent hissy fit.

1. CUTLERY SORT-OUT 2+ 🗩

If you've got a cutlery tray, tip all the forks, spoons and knives (the non-sharp ones, obvs) out on to a blanket. Pop the empty tray down beside the cutlery, then ask your little one to sort it all into the right place. I used to get Florence to do this while I emptied the dishwasher.

2. BEAR AND DOLL HOSPITAL 2+ ✂

A cheap packet of plasters can go a really long way! Get five dolls or teddies out, then make up five little beds using cushions and blankets. Grab a toilet roll, a box of plasters and a toy doctor's kit (if you have one), then let your little one tend to all the poorly toys.

3. PLAY DOUGH 2+ ✂

Grab a blob of play dough and five tools – either specific play-dough tools or safe kitchen utensils are fine. I've found a potato masher keeps kids occupied for a while. Using one colour of dough and just a handful of tools means there's limited mess. Plus two-year-olds don't yet have the attention span for spending hours on big creations, so you'll make your life easier by scaling things down for them.

4. WHACK-A-MOLE 2+ ⚽

Grab a medium-sized cardboard box, a toy and an inflated balloon. Cut five holes in the top of the box, then cut another one at the side. (The hole at the side is for you to reach your arm inside the box while holding the small toy, so you can make the toy pop out of the holes at the top.) Your little one has to try to hit the toy with the balloon. Swap over, so they have a turn poking the toy out of the holes while you do the whacking.

5. TEDDY BEARS' PICNIC 2+ 🗩

Lay a small blanket out on the ground, then sit five soft toys on it. If you have a tea set, get it out. If you don't, just use any suitable plates and cups. Add some toy food, if you have some, and you could also put water in the teapot to make cups of tea. Leave it for your little one to find!

There are some fabulous books out there that get readers to search for different-coloured things across the pages. We picked up a few secondhand – the book box at the charity shop is always worth a quick scour!

COLOURS

Colours can be a tricky thing to learn. Some children learn the name of one colour, then go through a phase of saying everything is that colour. Duck? Blue. Mummy? Blue. Wonderful. And it's just as you start panicking, thinking maybe your little one can't actually *see* colour, that they suddenly get it. So here are some fun rainbow games to play.

1. GUESS THE COLOUR

This is a good one for the paper hats you get in Christmas crackers, but if it isn't December just make a simple paper headband for your little one. Stick a bit of paper with a colour written or drawn on it to the hat or headband, then put it on your child's head. Now give your child clues about the colour, and they have to guess what it is. For example, say, 'This is the colour of a strawberry, and a London bus, and a clown's nose.' Let them be a colour detective!

2. COLOUR HUNT

Get five bits of paper and draw a different-coloured circle on each one. If you have binoculars, you could let your child use them, or just give them an empty toilet-roll 'telescope'. Tell them they need to hunt around the house for things that match each colour circle. How many things can they find for each colour? Which colour has the most things?

3. COLOUR PAIRS

Cut out ten squares of paper, then put them in five pairs. Scribble the same colour on each pair, and use a new colour for each pair. Now turn all the squares upside down, so you can't see the colours, and mix them up. You and your little one take turns choosing two squares at a time. Can you find a colour match? If you do, keep the pair. If not, put the squares back. The player with the most pairs at the end wins!

4. SIMON SAYS 'JUMP!'

Scribble five different colours on five different bits of paper, then put them around a room and play Simon Says. For example, if you say, 'Simon says jump on green!' your child must run and jump on green. Remind them that they only do what Simon says – if you just say 'jump on green' they have to stand still!

5. BLOCK TOWERS

If you have a box of coloured blocks, tip them all out. Then, on five bits of paper, draw five circles that match the colours of the blocks. Get your little one to build towers in each circle out of blocks that are the right colour.

Don't have a picnic blanket? Use an old fitted double sheet instead. Put your bags in the corners to create a little wall, which will minimize the sand where you're sitting. Winner.

ON THE BEACH

A sandy beach is basically a giant playground, isn't it? On a recent visit, the kids built and destroyed a hundred sandcastles, then swam in the sea and even drank it (in Florence's case – yuck!). I also cleaned up a beach turd (cheers, kiddo). It was only then that the wee ones started to get a bit bored. They found a dead crab, so while they were occupied with that I trotted off and drew up some sand games, which I then waited for them find.

1. NUMBER STEPPING STONES 3+ ⚽ 1²³

Write numbers in the sand, then draw circles round each one. For little ones, just write 1, 2 and 3. As they get the hang of it, you can gradually add more numbers. For older ones, draw the numbers all at funny angles and different distances. Tell your kids they have to hop into circles in the right order, then turn round and come back to the beginning without landing outside the circles – if they do, they'll get caught by the sharks! I shout 'Ding!' each time my kids get it right, then I let them shout numbers for me to jump on.

2. SAND TARGETS 2+ ⚽ 1²³

Draw a simple target in the sand, with three increasingly larger circles. Draw a line a few steps away from the target. Get each player to find a stone, then take it in turns to stand on the line and throw their stone at the target. If you like, you can tally scores.

3. MAKE THEM DISAPPEAR 3+ abc 1²³ ✎

Write letters in the sand with a stone. Can your wee ones rub them out faster than you can write them? My kids shuffled over the letters with their bare feet to rub them out, while I shouted the letters and sounds as I drew them. In the end I let them win by rubbing all the letters out. Then they had a go at writing while I rubbed their letters out!

4. RUBBISH COCONUT SHY 2+ ⚽

Grab some empty tin cans or bottles. Put a bit of sand in them, then sit them on top of little mounds of sand some distance away. Get your kids to go and collect lots of stones (which itself takes a while!). Then let them throw the stones to try to knock over the bottles or cans. The first to get them all wins! You could obviously also use a ball instead of stones.

5. THE CLASSICS 3+ ✎

Why not play noughts and crosses on the sand? This is a very simple one for slightly older kids. The best of five games wins, and the loser has to go and get the ice creams! Another classic you can play in the sand is hopscotch (see page 35).

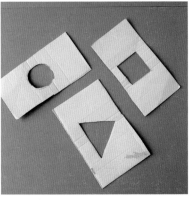

On days that drag, give the kids an early bath, put on your PJs and have a 'picnic tea' on a blanket in the lounge. My go–to for those days when I need to go straight to bed at the same time as they do!

SHAPES AND BLOCKS

Games that involve construction and shapes are really good for little brains. It might sound a bit complex to get children to build and problem-solve using shapes, but really it's just playing with blocks! One of the best things we own is a box of colourful wooden shapes – the games we can play with them are endless.

1. GIANT SHAPE-SORTER

If you have one, grab your box of different-shaped blocks. Make an outline of the different shapes in masking tape on the floor, as large as you can, and scatter the blocks around for the kids to sort into their matching masking-tape shapes. If you don't have blocks, simply make lots of shapes by drawing some on paper and cutting them out.

2. NUMBER TOWERS

Write a number on a bit of paper and draw a circle round it. Do this for as many numbers as your child can confidently manage. Then put the bits of paper on the floor and challenge your little one to build towers using the correct number of blocks for each. For older ones, you can write simple sums. For little ones, put the blocks into piles of the correct numbers, then get them to match the piles and numbers up.

3. GLOW-STICK SHAPES

Draw five shapes on paper, cut them out individually, then pop them into a bag. Get some glow sticks and make it dark. Ask your child to pick one shape out of the bag, then see if they can make that shape on the floor or in the air using their glow sticks.

4. SHAPE-FINDER

Draw some shapes on scraps of cardboard. Cut the shapes out so that each shape is a hole – you should be able to hold on to the cardboard and look through the shaped hole. These are your shape-finders. Give them to your little ones, and tell them to use the shape-finders to find things that match each shape. Show them how to look through their finders to do this. Get them to search around the house, or take their shape-finders on a walk. For example, for a circle they might find a button on the TV remote, or for a triangle they might find the letter A on a road sign. How many things can they find for each shape?

5. ROLL THE DICE

Grab a dice, a bit of paper and a pen. The idea with this one is to roll the dice, then match the number rolled to the number of sides a shape has – so if you roll a four that's a square, and if you roll a one that's a circle, and a two could be a semicircle or leaf shape. There are two ways to play: either draw the shapes on the paper first, then get your little one to roll the dice, count and match, or just roll the dice and ask your child to have a go at drawing the shapes themselves. Up to you!

If it's snowing, pop latex gloves over little woolly ones. This will stop your wee ones from getting wet, cold hands, which ruin all the snowman–building fun.

ENJOYING NATURE

Sometimes when you're desperate to get outdoors and escape the house the little blighters refuse to budge (or mine do, anyway). So, if I'm in the mood for some non-fart-scented air but they are digging in their heels, here are some of the things I do to entice them into the great outdoors.

1. CHOP IT UP 3+

If I've been out in the garden weeding or pruning, I just chuck everything on to a tray for each of the kids to explore with some scissors. It's actually quite satisfying to cut up petals and leaves, and you can get some excellent kid-friendly scissors.

2. COCONUT SHY 3+

When coconuts are cheap at the supermarket, I buy one for each of the kids. Outside at home, I pop each one on a cup, then give the kids a ball each to throw and knock off the coconut in front of them. Once they've won their coconut, I leave them to see if they can figure out how to crack it open. They'll spend a good five minutes dropping their coconut on to different surfaces.

3. PICNIC—PLATE DECORATING 2+

If we're heading out for a picnic, I like to give each of my kids a plain paper plate to decorate before we go. Not only is personalizing their plate a nice activity, but it also means I get left alone to pop sandwiches into bags.

4. MEDICINE SYRINGES 2+

In our bathroom cabinet, there's a cup filled with old medicine syringes left over from long nights of teething and temperatures. Grab a couple of clean ones and fill a cup with water, then leave everything in the garden for your kids to use to water the plants – or have a tiny water fight!

5. NATURE HUNT 3+

Draw or write the names of five natural items on a bit of paper – a leaf, a twig, a stone, etc. Then put a tick box next to each thing, and pop it by the door with an old gift bag alongside. Do this for each child. When your kids discover their lists, go outside on a nature hunt and get them to find all the items. This is a good one for playdates too!

I keep the small stuff like magnetic letters and numbers (and puzzles too) in large mesh pencil cases. They take up hardly any room in the cupboard and are easy to grab and pull out.

MAGNETIC LETTERS AND NUMBERS

These are the kinds of thing you buy because you think you should. Perhaps your child is preschool age, and you feel like magnetic letters and numbers would be excellent things to own? So you buy them – 'Good parent! Well done, me!' – then you stick them on the fridge. The kids show interest for thirty seconds, and then you're stuck and you wonder, 'Well, now what do we do?' Yep, I was also stumped at first. Here's what we came up with.

1. THE QUARRY 2+ 💬 abc 123

Set up a little train track or road. If you don't have either of these, use masking tape to make a road – you can even draw marker lines along the middle for added effect if you fancy! Make little piles of the letters at various points along the track or road. Put a baking tray at one end to use as a 'quarry'. Get a train, digger or a truck that can carry small items, then send your child off with it to collect the piles and bring them back to the quarry.

2. PLAY DOUGH STAMPS 3+ ⚽ abc 123

Roll out one piece of play dough and use the letters and numbers as stamps. For little ones just add them into their play and chat about the letters or numbers they can see. You could also stamp out their names by giving them the correct letters and seeing if they can put them in the right order. Or for older ones they could try words, spellings and sums. Way more fun than writing them down!

3. HIDE–AND–SEEK 3+ 💬 abc 123

Give each child ten letters. Tell them they have to find places in the house to stick the letters to and hide them from you. Once they've hidden them, you then go and find them – this gives you a chance to talk about what sorts of things are magnetic and what things are not. Alternatively hide the letters, then give your kids clues to find them by saying 'warmer' or 'colder'. If you have more than five minutes, you could even draw a little treasure map.

4. NAME THE TOY 3+ 💬 abc 123

Grab five toys, and give them all names (if they don't already have them). Get five paper clips or safety pins and attach one to each toy. Then ask your little ones to find the magnetic letter that matches the first letters of each toy's name. Once they get it right, they stick the letter to the clip or pin on the correct toy.

5. STAMPING 2+ abc 123

Did you know that letters and numbers that have a full magnetic backing can be used as stamps on Magna Doodles? Handy for your child to learn their name, spelling, phonics (see page 172) and tricky words. Mix up the order of the letters in words, and let your child correct you.

Like lots of folk, we have a cheeky elf who appears every year for advent – but instead of getting up to mischief, he brings a letter every day. On Christmas Eve, the letters spell out 'Father Christmas is coming tonight'. I know it's Christmas, kids, but letter learning can be festive too! (Especially if Mummy is hiding said letters after several glasses of Irish cream liqueur . . .)

CHRISTMAS

I mean, I hardly need to invent stuff for the wee ones to do over the madness that is December, do I? But a radio station once asked me to come up with some ideas for using all the tons of stuff that otherwise becomes waste around this time of year, and I wanted to include those ideas here.

1. CRACKER-TUBE SKITTLES 2+ ⚽

The insides of Christmas crackers are basically cardboard tubes. Collect six of them to use as skittles, then scrunch up a bit of used wrapping paper for a ball. Boom! A game for when the interest in the tiny plastic magnifying glass or photo frame has run out (i.e. within thirty seconds).

2. WRAP THAT 1+

Use leftover wrapping paper to make balls for Toddler Pong (page 115), Hip-shake Twerk Race (page 121) or Splat the Rat (page 31). You can also use it to wrap up puzzles or toys, then put them in a gift bag for your little one to explore.

3. GO HUNTING 2+ 💬

Turn those trusty Christmas-cracker tubes into a pair of binoculars by taping two together. Then grab some chocolate coins and hide them around the garden. Let your kids go out to search for the coins, while you scoff the tin of good chocolates in front of the TV inside, where it's warm. Mwah-ha-ha!

4. RETURN RUDOLPH'S NOSE 2+

Draw a simple Rudolph the Reindeer on a bit of scrap cardboard, then cut a little hole out where his nose should be. Get a red pom-pom or scrunch a bit of red wrapping paper into a small ball. Give your little one a straw, then see if they can blow the pom-pom or ball into the hole and return Rudolph's nose!

5. BUBBLE MAZE 2+ 💬

Draw five presents on a bit of paper, then draw a line between each one to create a 'maze'. Place the bit of paper in a plastic folder sellotaped shut or inside a ziplock bag, then pop it on a tray. Put lots of liquid soap and a splash of water into a bottle then shake it up to make bubbles. Squirt the bubble mixture over the top of the plastic-covered maze so you can't see it. Grab a small figurine – ideally a Santa – and a straw. Get your little one to blow the bubbles out of the way so that Santa can follow the maze, and find all the presents for his sleigh!

FIVE MINUTE FOOD AND DRINK HACKS

1. WINGS

If you give your little one a drink in a carton, lift the pointed flaps at the side of the carton to make wings! Tell your kiddo to always hold the carton by its wings, and you won't get the squeeze-and-spill. Especially handy on a summer's day. A juice-sodden toddler being swarmed by wasps is a surefire way to rapidly end an otherwise delightful picnic!

2. FRUIT

'Here, eat this bowl of fruit, kids.' Nope? That doesn't work here, either. Unless your child loves fruit (like Florence does), they won't be arsed (like Ewan). However, if you turn said fruit into a sword or a wand, it suddenly becomes quite enticing. Just pop it on to the end of a wooden kebab stick (with the pointy end snipped off). I also make a 'fruit fondue' by putting some yoghurt or chocolate sauce in an egg cup or a shot glass (those days are long gone!), then popping it in the middle of the bowl of fruit. Sprinkles added for extra encouragement!

3. HOMEMADE ICE LOLLIES

This is one of my favourite tricks. You can buy ice-lolly moulds from loads of places, and I fill mine with fresh juice. Then, whenever I need to hydrate the kids on a hot day or keep them quiet for five minutes or halt an impending meltdown, I say, 'Shall we have an ice lolly?' They think it's a treat, but really it's just a quarter of a cup of fruit juice. Guilt-free win! You can also make them with blended fruit and yoghurt, but I'm lazy so juice will do.

4. PANCAKE TOSSERS

We often make pancakes for breakfast at the weekend (one cup of plain flour, one cup of milk, one egg). The kids always want to toss them, so after I've finished cooking I give them a clean lightweight frying pan and pop a cooked pancake in it then let them toss away!

5. BANANA 'ICE CREAM'

If you blend frozen bananas with a splash of milk, it makes 'ice cream'. Really handy if you've got bananas in the fruit bowl that are about to go past their best. Just peel them, chop them up and stick them in the freezer in a container or ziplock bag, then whack them in the blender when you need them. For extra flavour, add chocolate spread, peanut butter or vanilla essence. When the kids say, 'Yum,' you can do the lesser spotted smug face.

MAKING A SONG AND DANCE

We love to end the day with a kitchen disco. There is something so free and joyful about dancing with kids. Although, the kids are hidden beneath the windowsill in our front room, so if any neighbours walk past while we're having a boogie it'll just look like me rocking out on my own. Excellent.

HERE ARE SOME OF THE SONGS WE LIKE TO FINISH THE DAY WITH (A.K.A. 'LET'S WEAR THE KIDS OUT BEFORE BEDTIME'):

1. 'Superman' by Black Lace: A song where the lyrics are all actions so everyone can join in! My two love it when it goes double fast at the end.

2. 'I am the Music Man' by Black Lace: Ditto.

3. 'Agadoo' by Black Lace: You can basically just type 'Black Lace' into YouTube and dance along!

4. 'The Hokey Cokey': Put your legs and arms in and out and shake them all about. Easy.

5. 'Head, Shoulders Knees and Toes': A classic. Do the actions with the kids, and get faster and faster until you all collapse in a heap of giggles.

It goes without saying that Disney songs are a frequent feature in our house – sometimes just for Mummy to sing along to! All together now: 'Let it gooooo!'

IS FIVE MINUTES ENOUGH?

Five little minutes.
That's all.
Set a timer.

If you're sitting down for the first time today, you'll find it goes really quickly. By contrast, it'll go really slowly if your baby is crying at full volume and you're in an enclosed and crowded space. (Yes, I'm thinking of that flight from Malaga which we foolishly missed, then had to pay double for another one and ended up with a cranky and overtired Ewan all the way home! Argh!)

But is spending five minutes playing enough? Yes. It is.

If you've spent those five minutes with your little one, giving them your full and undivided attention, then it's perfect. And it doesn't have to be playing one of the games in this book, either.

How often should you play for five minutes? Well, that depends.

What I mean by 'five minutes' is 'five minutes at a time'. If I am home with the kids all day long, then I aim to play a five-minute game like the ones in this book twice a day – once in the morning, and once in the afternoon.

The rest of the time, I break it down. I make sure we read for five minutes, either at bedtime or over breakfast. Alternatively, I chuck a load of books that the kids haven't seen for a while out on the floor. I'll also spend five minutes doing something with them that they enjoy, such as playing hide-and-seek. We'll spend five minutes chatting or cuddling or rolling around on the floor tickling until everyone is red in the face from laughing. I'll spend five minutes dancing in the kitchen. I'll dedicate five minutes to asking them to tidy up (usually futile, but worth a try). And, of course, the TV and tablets are for when we've all had enough.

The leftover time is filled in with the rest of the shizzle we have to do as parents. Getting them dressed, going to the shops, emptying the dishwasher while they play/ fight, cooking meals, putting on MORE washing. There is a big, long never-ending list that grown-up parenting requires; we all know it, and it is so easy to get lost in it. There's always something else demanding your attention. It's exhausting.

If you work outside the home and your time with your little one is limited, then you can use these five-minute games to maximize the time you do have. One of the kicks I really needed to start my blog was helping out a wonderful friend of mine who is a cardiologist. Full-time life saver and full-time mummy of two. She wanted to support her little ones with nursery learning, but she needed it to be fast and easy to fit around shift patterns and rushing home for bath time. I designed lots of these games with her in mind. Whether you're a working parent or a stay-at-home one, your job comes with challenges – they're just of a different nature. We all need it to be quick and easy.

I have never sat my kids down at a table and said, 'Let's learn some letters,' or, 'Right, we are going write all our numbers from one to ten now.' We've only ever played five-minute games. Every day. Little and often. Ewan skipped off to school confidently recognizing most letters and numbers up to ten. But is that what made me happy? No. It was knowing how much FUN we'd had learning it all. The constant laughter and the wide-eyed expression of joy on his face whenever he figured something out will be forever imprinted on my brain. I give my kids five so they give me five.

Time is limited, so it needs to be spent joyfully together. Fun should always be the priority. I hope this book brings you that in abundance.

Five minutes is all you need. It's enough.
Those minutes add up.
Put down the phone,
the laptop,
the marigolds.
Set something up today. I promise, it really is enough.

ACKNOWLEDGEMENTS

Firstly I'd just like to thank the incredible team at Penguin Random House Children's for all your support in helping me pull this book together. When I felt out of my depth you kept me afloat. Huge thanks also to my literary agent Lauren Gardner who was the first person to say to me (aside from friends and family who are obliged to!) 'I think you could write a book' and push me to actually go ahead and do it.

A big thank-you to these wonderful women, a powerhouse of awesome fellow mums who supported my blog from the very off, listened to me bang on about it, read it, shared it, but most importantly played the games with the little ones in their lives so that I knew I was on to something . . . Jo Howley, Nic Majekodunmi, Michaela Pashley, Gemma Souders, Hannah Ascott, Rebecca Harvey, Claire Blackburn, Jenny Upton, Natalie Hancock, Kelly Morel, Emma Rawlinson, Jasmine Hughes, Nat Jeffrey and Jenna Andrews. Your backing kept me going. Also a wee hat tip to #fivehourdad Nick Ascott.

Gratitude always to Elizabeth Sanders for her online wisdom, Sneha Patel for being my rock when I was jelly-legged and Danielle Lewis-Collins for always making time for me no matter what.

My little gang of online buddies cheerleading me through the strange and magical world of social media . . . Gina, Chara, Abbie, Hannah and Becky – cheers. You inspire me, support me but most of all make me laugh and for that, I will never unfollow you! ;)

Big thanks also to Sarah 'Unmumsy' Turner for her ongoing support and advice on the blog-to-book whirlwind, and for providing a cover quote. I was just chuffed you even followed me!

A massive thank-you to Grandad Willie, who was the one doing pick-ups and drop-offs and keeping the wee bairns busy while I was typing away. We feel so lucky to have you as part of our family.

And to my wonderful husband, Kenny. Thank you for always stepping in when I need it most. For getting up early every day. For tolerating the games testing chaos and me sat with my phone and laptop for hours on end. For coming up with my new persona and for always believing in me and my mad project. Does this count as a 'paper' gift for our one-year wedding anniversary?

I didn't do a speech at my wedding so I want to take this rare opportunity to properly thank my mum and dad, Jennie and Cliff. No matter what I do in life they are always there. Pushing me on with unswerving support and hovering with a safety net, should I need it. The biggest testament I feel I can give them is to say that I still, always, love to be in their company, and truly wish that in the future my own children feel the same way about me. Thank you so much for everything you do and have done. Now I'm a parent too, I get it, and can only hope me telling you how much I love you both in a book makes up for all the bum-wiping and tantrum-throwing I put you through!

But the biggest and final thank-you has to go to two little ones without whom this book wouldn't exist, Ewan and Florence. The best games testers I could ever wish for. There aren't two people in the whole world I would rather spend five minutes with than you both. I love you with everything I've got and always will, and am so grateful to you for being such superstars while Mummy puts all our silly games down on paper to share with the world. I hope this book forever reminds us of all the brilliant fun we've had.

INDEX

ABOUT THE AUTHOR

Daisy Upton is a Londoner who now lives in Cheshire with her husband and two children. After years of working in sports broadcasting, she quit her job to become a teaching assistant, which her colleagues at the time found baffling! When her two children turned three and one, she found that her love of coming up with silly games to make learning more fun finally came into its own at home, and she began blogging about what she was up to. It turned out that quite a few other people wanted to play these games too. Daisy now has a large social media and blog following, who share with her on a daily basis how they too are playing her games. Daisy likes to celebrate this fact by eating large quantities of chocolate oranges and Creme Eggs (season dependent), and dancing in the kitchen.

 @fiveminutemum

 fiveminutemumma

@fiveminutemum

www.fiveminutemum.com